FUNDAMENTALS

OF

SOCIOLOGY OF SPORT AND PHYSICAL ACTIVITY

Human Kinetics' Fundamentals of Sport and Exercise Science Series

Katherine M. Jamieson, PhD
California State University, Sacramento

Maureen M. Smith, PhD
California State University, Sacramento

HUMAN KINETICS

Library of Congress Cataloging-in-Publication Data

Names: Jamieson, Katherine M., 1965- author. | Smith, Maureen, 1967- author.
Title: Fundamentals of sociology of sport and physical activity / Katherine
   M. Jamieson, Maureen Smith.
Description: Champaign, IL : Human Kinetics, [2016] | Series: Human Kinetics'
   fundamentals of sport and exercise science series | Includes
   bibliographical references and index.
Identifiers: LCCN 2016007936 | ISBN 9781450421027 (print)
Subjects: LCSH: Sports--Sociological aspects. | Physical
   fitness--Sociological aspects. | Physical education and
   training--Sociological aspects.
Classification: LCC GV706.5 .J365 2016 | DDC 306.4/83--dc23 LC record available at https://lccn.loc.gov/2016007936

ISBN: 978-1-4504-2102-7 (print)

The web addresses cited in this text were current as of May 2016, unless otherwise noted.

Senior Acquisitions Editor: Myles Schrag; Developmental Editor: Ragen E. Sanner; Managing Editor: Karla Walsh; Copyeditor: Joy Hoppenot; Indexer: Gerry Lynn Shipe; Permissions Manager: Dalene Reeder; Graphic Designer: Whitney Milburn; Cover Designer: Keith Blomberg; Photographs (interior): © Human Kinetics, unless otherwise noted. Photo on p. 33 reprinted from Rose Physical Therapy Group, 2014, District Crossfit Class Warfare. This file is licensed under the Creative Commons Attribution 2.0. https://commons.wikimedia.org/wiki/File:District_Crossfit_Class_Warfare-47_%2814973829717%29.jpg; Photo Asset Manager: Laura Fitch; Photo Production Manager: Jason Allen; Senior Art Manager: Kelly Hendren; Illustrations: © Human Kinetics; Printer: Versa Press

Printed in the United States of America   10 9 8 7 6 5 4 3 2 1

The paper in this book is certified under a sustainable forestry program.

Human Kinetics
Website: www.HumanKinetics.com

United States: Human Kinetics
P.O. Box 5076
Champaign, IL 61825-5076
800-747-4457
e-mail: info@hkusa.com

Canada: Human Kinetics
475 Devonshire Road Unit 100
Windsor, ON N8Y 2L5
800-465-7301 (in Canada only)
e-mail: info@hkcanada.com

Europe: Human Kinetics
107 Bradford Road
Stanningley
Leeds LS28 6AT, United Kingdom
+44 (0) 113 255 5665
e-mail: hk@hkeurope.com

Australia: Human Kinetics
57A Price Avenue
Lower Mitcham, South Australia 5062
08 8372 0999
e-mail: info@hkaustralia.com

New Zealand: Human Kinetics
P.O. Box 80
Mitcham Shopping Centre, South Australia 5062
0800 222 062
e-mail: info@hknewzealand.com

E5592

Contents

Series Preface

The sport sciences have matured impressively over the past 50 years. Subdisciplines in kinesiology have established their own rigorous paths of research, and physical education in its many forms is now an accepted discipline in higher education. Our need now is not only for comprehensive resources that contain all the knowledge that the field has acquired, but also for resources that summarize the foundations of each of the sport sciences for the variety of people who make use of that information today. Understanding the basic topics, goals, and applications of the subdisciplines in kinesiology is critical for students and professionals in many walks of life. Human Kinetics has developed the Fundamentals of Sport and Exercise Science series with these needs in mind.

This and the other books in the series will not provide you with all the in-depth knowledge required for earning an advanced degree or for opening a practice in this subject area. Other books in Human Kinetics' Fundamentals Sport and Exercise Science series include the following:

- *Fundamentals of Sport and Exercise Psychology* by Alan Kornspan
- *Fundamentals of Sport and Exercise Nutrition* by Marie Dunford
- *Fundamentals of Motor Behavior* by Jeffrey Fairbrother
- *Fundamentals of Sport Management* by Robert Baker and Craig Esherick

Key to Icons

Look for the giant quotation marks, which set off noteworthy quotes from researchers and professionals in the field.

Quick Facts include quirky or surprising "Did you know?" types of information.

Success Stories highlight influential individuals in the field. Through these sidebars, you will learn how researchers and professionals apply their knowledge of the subject to their work, and you'll be able to explore possible career paths in the field.

Using Your Sociological Imagination sidebars ask questions to get you to use a sociological perspective and discover how sociology can be applied to physical activity and sports.

Time Capsules describe moments in time when sociology was influenced by physical activity and sports.

This book will not make you an expert on the subject. What this book will do is give you an excellent grounding in the key themes, terms, history, and status of the subject in both the academic and professional worlds. You can use this grounding as a jumping-off point for studying more in-depth resources and for generating questions for more experienced people in the field. We've even included a list of additional resources for you to consult as you continue your journey.

You might be using this book to help you improve your professional skills or to assess the potential job market. You might want to learn about a new subject, supplement a textbook, or introduce a colleague or client to this exciting subject area. In any of these cases, this book will be your guide to the basics of this subject. It is succinct, informative, and entertaining. You will begin the book with many questions, and you will surely finish it with many more questions. But they will be more thoughtful, complex, and substantive questions. We hope that you will use this book to help the sport sciences, and this subject in particular, continue to prosper for another generation.

Preface

Fundamentals of Sociology of Sport and Physical Activity offers a chance to consider sport, exercise, and physical education beyond the physical realm. All human physical activity occurs within a larger social, cultural, and even political context. Understanding what this means and how this takes shape is a crucial aspect of kinesiology, or the field formerly known as physical education. Whether you are a fan, participant, parent, teacher, athletic trainer, or just an avid reader, you will gain insight to the ways that the humanities and social sciences, specifically sociology and cultural studies, are crucial to a deep understanding of the value and place of physical activity in society. The book should pique your interest in the mundane, taken-for-granted aspects of sport, exercise, and physical education.

As in the broader context of sociocultural analyses, the book focuses on societal-level issues, problems, structures, and values. No single book can bring the humanities and physical activity into full view, but the aim here is to generate basic understanding and ongoing interest in sociocultural questions around physical activity. Ongoing questions for social scientists in kinesiology focus on issues of equity, such as patterns of participation across social categories of race, class, gender, sexuality, and ability; physical activity in various spheres of daily life like school, church, and family settings; dominant cultural values and messages about physical activity, especially as delivered through the mass media, health and sport organizations, and youth development programs; and advocacy for a more physically active society. An introduction to sociological and cultural studies analyses partnered with examples of current societal-level issues will surely invite you to formulate new questions and ideas about human movement as more than physical and to recognize how sport and physical activity already reflect dominant cultural ideas and conditions.

This book recognizes that sport and physical activity are deeply connected to our daily lives. Even if we are not sports fans or elite athletes, it is difficult, if not impossible, to get through a day without some encounter with sport or physical activity. In fact, throughout this book, we focus on sporting spaces, schooling spaces, and exercising spaces, just to highlight a few of the ways that human movement shapes our daily lives. For example, every two years we are treated to an international mega-sporting event, the Olympic Games. For two weeks, we witness elite human performance as well as nations trying to demonstrate superiority. We may also recall school-based physical education, where we may have experienced success and failure and learned physical as well as social skills. Exercise settings may also hold insights for us about the social world, especially in very social settings like fitness centers, community fun runs, or the new competitive fitness realm of CrossFit.

Because the social sciences pose deep questions about our everyday, taken-for-granted social interactions, it can sometimes feel uncomfortable, difficult, and overly critical—it is all these things. The discomfort comes in part from engaging in a type of questioning and knowledge production that is new to most people interested in physical activity. It is also discomforting for most of us to learn how to value and apply sociocultural critique to something we would rather simply enjoy and love—physical activity. Yet, time and again, it is clear that asking critical questions and engaging in what some scholars call a loving critique of our field of study are the best way to advance meaningful physical activity for all citizens. Social scientists in physical activity and other fields of study take very seriously their role in identifying, naming, and critiquing existing social structures; related hierarchies of access, power, and control; and opportunities for physical activity to play a significant role in desired and required social change. This book provides an entry point to these crucial conversations and professional endeavors.

The book is divided into two parts. Part I provides a background to the discipline-specific knowledge in the social and cultural analysis of physical activity, including a description of the development of the field and its professional organizations, publications, and opportunities for professional practice. Part II engages you in key issues in particular sporting spaces. Research findings and key questions in the field are discussed as they relate to each of three common social spaces for physical activity: sporting spaces, exercising spaces, and schooling spaces.

Acknowledgments

I am forever thankful for the many people and animal friends in my life who have led me to believe that my ideas and my presence in the world matter. To my family—especially Amy, Mom, and Terry—I say thanks for understanding how much time and mind space it takes for me to write and for loving me unconditionally in my absence and presence along the way. To my mentors—especially Dr. Diane Ross, Dr. Yvonne R. Smith, and Dr. Maxine Baca Zinn—I say a special thank-you for teaching me how to feed my own thirst for knowledge in ways that are bigger than me and hopefully contribute meaningfully to a greater whole. I am also thankful to so many colleagues who graciously listen to and critique new ideas around teaching, research, and service commitments toward our grand belief in an impactful democratic educational project. Among these colleagues is my coauthor, Dr. Maureen Smith, who has made this project a much more timely, provocative, and nuanced analysis and has added the important element of fun to our collaborative labor. At the core of this book is nearly 20 years of challenging and thoughtful striving by so many students with whom I have had the pleasure to learn and grow, especially around questions of meaningful human movement. Special thanks to the folks at Human Kinetics, especially Myles Schrag and Ragen Sanner, for support in key developmental moments of the project, and to Yeomi Choi, Laura Pipe, and Casey Casas for reading early drafts of chapters and assistance with image searches. Finally, I am confident that my intellectual analyses of human movement emerge not only from textbooks but also from having deeply felt what it is to move (in the midst of freedom, in constraint, and all contexts in between). Thus, I am eternally thankful for all the miles I have been able to run, walk, bike, hike, and kayak on lands that are not my own.

Katherine M. Jamieson

I am indebted to the good will and generosity of my friend and colleague (and favorite ABA player) Dr. J for inviting me to join her project. Talking about, thinking about, and writing about how we teach have been fun and rewarding and have resulted in many edits to my own course notes, assignments, and lectures. I was fortunate to have two teachers and mentors at Ithaca College who fostered my love of looking at sport from a critical perspective, Dr. Deb Wuest and Dr. Steve Mosher. Drs. Wuest and Mosher exemplified the pursuit of excellence in teaching and provided me guidance to follow the academic path. I have been a faculty member for over 20 years at California State University, Sacramento, where teaching is our primary purpose. We have plenty of opportunities to practice our craft with a teaching load that demands much of us. I am so lucky to get to share the classroom with amazing students who engage with the ideas and materials—and whose feedback over the years has helped shape this book. Finally, friends and colleagues in NASSS, NASSH, and ISHPES have shared their materials, ideas, and assignments and continually serve as terrific models of professionals who continue to strive to serve their students in the classroom. Many thanks to all. As our discipline continues to evolve and the sporting world expands, I am more convinced than ever that we could all benefit from working on our sociological imagination.

Maureen M. Smith

I

PART

Introduction to the Sociology of Sport and Physical Activity

Part I of *Fundamentals of Sociology of Sport and Physical Activity* offers an overview of the academic field most commonly known as the sociology of sport, including its origins related to other fields of study and deep ties to physical education and sociology, as well as professional practice in the field. Chapter 1 describes the historical roots and development of the field and introduces the work of sociologists of sport and physical activity, especially around the various ways that sport and physical activity programs play a role in the daily functioning of society. Chapter 2 offers a glimpse into the varied ways that various types of professionals put sociological knowledge to use. This chapter also outlines the educational requirements for professional practice and manner of generating sociological knowledge around sport and physical activity. Together, these chapters orient you to a discipline that advances a critique of sport and physical activity in an effort to enhance the social contributions and accessibility of sport, physical education, and exercise for all members of society.

CHAPTER 1

What Is Sociology of Sport and Physical Activity?

In this chapter you will learn the following:

✓ Aspects of the field of sociology of sport and physical activity

✓ Why sociology is important and relevant to the study of sport and physical activity

✓ How the field developed over time

✓ What a sociologist of sport and physical activity does

✓ Who ought to apply a sociological lens to sport and physical activity

[T]he generation of [sociological] research questions . . . are not solely the responsibility of the researcher. Rather, the responsibility must be shared by all who teach, coach, and are involved in the study of human movement.

Susan L. Greendorfer (1977, p. 64)

Can you imagine being the best athlete in your high school and not being allowed on the team? That was the situation for Hall of Fame golfer Nancy Lopez, who had to stand before the school board and demand her right to participate on the boys' golf team because her school did not have a girls' team. Imagine as well that your father is your coach and your mother takes on additional work to ensure you can keep playing golf. Your parents do these things not only because they share an interest in your development but also because the sport of golf is more expensive than your family's income can accommodate, and the local country club has no visible non-White members. Thus, your family is your primary resource for the sport of golf. These were also characteristics of the elite athletic journey of Nancy Lopez. Add to this that once Lopez made it to the Ladies Professional Golf Association (LPGA) tour in 1978, there were questions about her authenticity as a person of Mexican descent, her frequent weight gains and losses, and her role as a wife, mother, and professional athlete. We could use Nancy Lopez's life to describe the goals and value of sociological analyses in sport and physical activity. In fact, it would be difficult to know about these intricacies of Lopez's own physical cultural journey unless you were a longtime dedicated fan of Lopez or if you had an interest in sociological, historical, and cultural questions about sport and physical activity.

This story of Nancy Lopez, like so many other sport stories, is important to consider sociologically for a number of reasons. First and foremost, sport and physical activity have been crucial interaction points for human beings throughout recorded history. Some scholars suggest that what we now know as sport and even play began as necessary activities of daily life, often tied to meeting basic needs such as gathering food, educating new members of society, and engaging in ritual recognition and celebration. In some ways, meeting her basic needs was at the core of Nancy Lopez's experience—she wasn't hunting and gathering and dancing for ritual, but she was asking a powerful group to grant her access to a resource that would change her **life chances**. For sociologists, the term *life chances* refers to the likelihood of encountering and being able to use various types of resources in the social world that aid in crafting a well-appointed life. The popular phrase "the rich get richer" reflects the notion that the conditions of life into which we are born will most certainly influence our ability to change that life or create a preferred life. Sport and physical activity are also worthy of sociological attention because they are active elements of our economy, consumer behavior, and entertainment activities, and they have the ability to affect life chances for many of us. Chapter 2 discusses this in more detail, but the point is that sport is present in our daily lives, even if we are not athletes ourselves. In fact, sport has value for athletes, fans, community and friendship groups, parents of kids in physical education (PE) and sport, weekend exercisers, and many others.

Knowledge in the sociology of sport and physical activity would allow you not only to marvel at Lopez's elite athletic performance but more importantly to understand her accomplishments in a broader social context. Using Lopez's **physical cultural** story, you could investigate important questions about sport and social difference like race, social class, sexuality and gender, sport and family systems, fandom, sport as work and athletes as workers, and even sport and nationalism. You, of course, could raise similar questions about other sport personalities and maybe even about yourself or people you know. In doing so, you would be applying a sociological lens to sport and physical activity. This would require the sensibilities described previously. More specifically, as Mills (1959/2004) suggested, historical, comparative, and structural sensitivity are each required for a comprehensive and wide-open **sociological imagination**. This three-pronged curiosity is a great starting point for thinking about sport and physical activity in society, but as you will see in this chapter and in chapter 2, it takes dedicated study in order to truly develop a sociological imagination and to apply your sociological lens.

Acquiring a sociological imagination, or what others might simply refer to as developing a sociological perspective, requires at its core a desire, willingness, and ability to shift focus from one's personal and immediate experience in order to observe that experience as part of larger social patterns. This ability is what Mills referred to as the ability to fully grasp the relations between history and biography. For example, as many of the reports produced by the Institute for Diversity and Ethics in Sport indicate, professional sport settings continue to have a glass ceiling for women and people of color. To quote Mills, "When, in a city of 100,000, only one [person] is unemployed that is their personal trouble . . . but when, in a nation of 50 million employees, 15 million [people] are unemployed that is an issue" (2004, p. 4). The sociological imagination suggests that troubles are micro or local issues affecting people in unique ways, while *issues* are reflective of the broader organizational structure of society. Mills posed three core questions: "What is the structure of this particular society as a whole?" "Where does this society stand in human history?" and "What variety of [people] now prevail in this society and in this period?" (1959/2004, p. 3). In doing so, Mills invited

life chances—A term introduced by sociologist Max Weber that refers to the likelihood that people may improve their quality of life.

physical culture—An academic and intellectual focus on the social and cultural meanings of human physical activity.

sociological imagination—A term introduced by C. Wright Mills in 1959 to draw attention to the need and capacity for human beings to make sense of their personal life stories and the larger patterns of changing societal conditions.

sport—An organized competitive game that takes place within a broad range of formality and governance.

cultural—Reflective of beliefs, practices, and ways of life.

Title IX—A U.S. law, first passed in 1972, requiring gender equity in federally funded educational settings, including sport.

all citizens to increase their capacity for understanding and cocreating the social world in which they wish to live. Consider the rapid change that has occurred in your lifetime. Mills was also responding to significant social change in the United States and the world in the 1950s. He wasn't trying to recruit sociologists or define the field of sociology; he was making sociological knowledge useful in everyday life, especially in a rapidly changing world.

Other scientific fields like psychology remain focused on individual performance-related experiences. In contrast, social scientists constantly try to make sense of societal components that are external to the individual yet greatly influence the ways people can interact in their social worlds. These societal components are typically observed as major spheres of life, such as the economy, politics, mass media, education, and religion, as well as in historical and cultural contexts or dominant currents of thought and societal norms. Social scientists typically focus their attention in some way on one or more of the three components that make up Mills' sociological imagination and on the ways that these components influence individual social context and human interaction.

Like Mills, we encourage readers to develop the skills and informed intellect to ask questions that place their personal experiences into articulation with larger social patterns, especially in reaching beyond opinion about the social contours of their physically active life. For example, you go to a CrossFit gym near your home and notice that middle-aged women often ask for more coaching and instruction in weightlifting techniques than the men in the same age group do. Observing individual women as deficient in their weight-training knowledge would be a limited perspective. A sociological imagination or perspective might lead you to ponder the historical and cultural context of physical education and sport for women and men, to imagine the varied social motives undergirding these human explorations of new sport skills, and to consider the social norms around physical culture for adult women and men that may support or challenge engagement in weight training. This is not to say that these women in your gym do not also have deeply personal experiences that shape their approach to physical activity, but your sociological perspective will tell you that even those deeply personal experiences are always already tied to larger patterns of interaction in the social world.

We define **sport** as a wide range of human physical activity that encompasses contexts of play, competition, and even paid labor (e.g., professional sport). From our perspective, sport is a significant and ever-present sphere of social life that invites a range of human interactions among participants, league officials, fans, business owners, politicians, and many others. It is also clear to us that sport is a moving

Quick Fact

Sixty percent of the 10 million self-proclaimed CrossFitters identify as female (Babiash, Porcari, Steffen, Doberstein, & Foster, 2013).

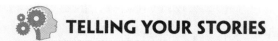

TELLING YOUR STORIES

Turn the sociological lens on yourself or someone you know.

1. What might you learn about society and larger social issues by simply asking a friend, "Tell me the story of physical activity in your life"?

2. What questions might you ask if you want to go deeper?

3. How is the story of physical activity in your life tied to broader social and historical structures and contexts?

target, or an ever-evolving social sphere of human interaction. What counts as sport today may not be the same 10 years from now—consider Quidditch, snowboarding, and CrossFit. Ten years ago, these sports were not sanctioned or even formally organized. Today, each of these is uniquely organized and governed by formal sport organizations. Our definition of sport and what we believe to be its core definition in the field of sociology of sport are intentionally fluid. Sport sociologists focus on the varied meanings that different social groups bring to their physical activity involvement in particular historical moments.

Sport and Physical Activity as Cultural Context

Understanding sport as more than physical—as also **cultural**—is a requirement for anyone interested in applying a sociological analysis to human movement. Regardless of what sport or physical activity setting you choose to study, you will encounter and even learn to desire origin stories. That is, it is common to want to identify the beginning of something and the official reasoning behind its development. Review of various types of research on specific sporting moments indicates that origin stories are never complete—they tell a partial, agreed-upon tale of the beginning. For this reason, we suggest that the sociology of sport and physical activity has many origins and has emerged out of varied interests, histories, moments, and events in human physical culture.

For example, in the Lopez story, one might want to imagine that all women were liberated through sport with the passage of **Title IX**—the educational amendment that made school-based sport available to girls in federally funded schools. Title IX is a U.S. law passed in 1972 requiring gender equity for boys and girls in every educational program that receives federal funding. It is intriguing to imagine all girls and women being equally, universally liberated in the same moment by a historic change like the passage of Title IX, but this is not how it worked out. In fact, the law has had many starts and stops in its application since 1972. It has become most known for its work in sport settings but more recently is gaining attention around educational opportunities in science, technology, engineering, and mathematics. It took many schools more than 10 years to implement Title IX, with some changes coming very slowly despite the law's passage. The fact that Lopez had to fight a

kinesiology—The study of human movement.

sociology—The study of human interaction and social structures.

national-level equity battle in a local way suggests that even when formal policy and law are in place, they are incomplete, and our democracy requires citizens to actively seek social justice. The Lopez story advances the idea that sport and physical activity are important sites for enacting democracy, seeking social justice, and reflecting current cultural beliefs and values.

In fact, any observation of sport and or physical activity reveals various social practices and values. Even a casual observer of informal play among young people in the United States can note values and beliefs about leadership, symbols of success, preferred ways to achieve, and various social hierarchies around age, gender, and ability. For example, many youth sport leagues hand out medals to winners of sporting events, while other leagues provide every participant with a certificate (or sometimes a medal) of participation. These are two different approaches to recognizing athletes: One values talent and winning and the other participation. You might even watch children as they choose teams, with girls often being picked after boys, better athletes before less-skilled athletes, and older before younger. These practices and values change over time and by place, further revealing connections in historical, sociological, and philosophical understandings of physical activity.

At present, the sociology of sport and physical activity is best known as an academic discipline with roots in both kinesiology and sociology. As the study of human movement, **kinesiology** fits well with **sociology**, which is the study of human social behavior. But, rest assured, you don't need to earn a doctoral degree to develop an interest in and value for sociological analyses of sport and physical activity. Even for those who do choose to develop the research and inquiry skills of a social scientist, the most meaningful sociological questions about human movement often emerge from everyday interactions and careful, consistent observations. This is not a science contained in a laboratory. In fact, society and the various social spaces of physical activity become your laboratory if your interest is in sociology of sport and physical activity. It is also highly likely that you already have relevant knowledge and experiences with sociological issues as well as with other bodies of knowledge. Even if you do not yet feel a deep understanding or resonance with sociological knowledge, read on. What you encounter here will aid you in learning to look differently at sport and physical activity.

As you continue, beware, since the application of social science knowledge may cause you to question your everyday sense of the world and the things you take for granted. This approach may feel uncomfortable, difficult, and even overly critical. The discomfort comes in part from engaging in a type of questioning and knowledge production that is new to most people, as well as facing our many possible roles in society—learning to be a fully engaged, socially aware citizen is daunting. It is also discomforting for most of us to learn how to apply sociocultural critique to something we enjoy and love—sport and physical activity. In a way, applying a social science perspective to sport and physical activity takes away a sort of innocence and the goodwill we imagine in all physical activity settings. Yet, as Eitzen (2012) so clearly suggested, it is in posing critical questions that we are able to imagine physically active communities that are fully accessible to all citizens.

 TITLE IX

In 1972, Congress passed Title IX, which states, "No person in the United States shall, on the basis of sex, be excluded from participation in, be denied the benefits of, or be subjected to discrimination under any education program or activity receiving federal financial assistance" (Title IX, Education Amendments of 1972, section 1681, para. 1). At the time, only 1 in 27 high school girls participated in high school sports. Now, more than 1 in 3 girls in high school play sports, and female athletes receive college scholarships in more than 20 sports. However, less than 50 percent of college athletic budgets are allocated to women's sports, and many colleges fail to meet the basic standards of Title IX. Moreover, in 1972, most girls' teams were coached by women; today, over 50 percent of girls' and women's teams are coached by men. This indicates that the stature of girls' and women's athletics has increased but also points to the challenges faced by women who would like to pursue coaching as a profession. Women coach less than 2 percent of boys' and men's teams.

Since the passage of Title IX, more than a third of girls in high school play sports.

While gender equity seems a basic principle in the United States, when faced with budget constraints, many athletic directors blame Title IX rather than admit that they simply value men's sports more than women's sports. More precisely, they value revenue-generating male sports more than non-revenue-generating male and female sports. However, at the high school and college levels, one argument for the inclusion of athletics is about the educational experience. This negates the argument that revenue sports are more important than non-revenue sports. The following timeline indicates the ongoing mixed feelings and sporadic support for enforcement of Title IX (The MARGARET Fund of NWLC, n.d.):

- 1972 President Richard M. Nixon signs the title into law.
- 1974 The Department of Health, Education and Welfare drafts regulations for enacting the law.
- 1976 First compliance deadline for elementary schools.
- 1978 First compliance deadline for secondary schools and colleges and universities.
- 1984 The law is established as ineffective in sport settings (due to "direct fed $").
- 1988 The law is deemed effective in sport again (new language).
- 1996 First Equity in Athletics Disclosure Act reports due.

sociology of sport—An area of academic study with links to the social sciences and the field of kinesiology.

subdiscipline—An area of study underlying an overarching academic field or disciplinary area of study.

Social scientists in physical activity and other fields of study take very seriously their role in identifying, naming, and critiquing existing social structures; related hierarchies of access, power, and control; and opportunities for physical activity to play a significant role in desired or required social change. The sociocultural study of sport and physical activity is one pathway to these crucial conversations and professional endeavors.

In table 1.1, we ask you to think about the different approaches and questions the social sciences and natural sciences bring to various movement settings. You can see that the different disciplines are all interested in movement yet have vastly different questions related to movement.

Origins and Key Movements

Sociology of sport is most typically identified as a **subdiscipline** in the field of kinesiology. The term *subdiscipline* refers to a crucial aspect of the overarching discipline, sort of like a spoke in a wheel, a branch of a tree, or a menu item on your digital gaming system. Sociological sport analysis emerged as a crucial sphere of kinesiology (previously known as physical education) in the 1960s. Of course, it also emerged from the field of sociology, but it has been met with contention given its perceived alignment with fun and games rather than with the serious aspects of daily life.

Ironically, a Protestant work ethic could be blamed for the successful promotion of personal and social responsibility for productive physical activity as well as for the sociological preference for the study of true labor and thus disaffection for the study of sport and physical activity (Rice, 1929). Again, utilizing a sociological imagination, sociologist Max Weber suggested that the Protestant Reformation, or the ethical rejection of the belief in a salvation that was possible only through one's church, offered support to the core values of capitalism. Simply stated, the belief that people could ensure a meaningful life through hard work and ethical living offered a significant cultural shift in terms of identifying the places and ways people could do "good work." Taking good care of one's God-given body became one component of this cultural shift. As a result, all things secular, or not affiliated with religious practice, became open to judgments about their capacity for moral behavior, including all forms of physical activity such as play, games, and sport. Reflecting on this interesting societal shift, sociological analysis of sport and physical activity in North

TABLE 1.1   Social Science and Natural Science Approaches

Sporting space	Social science	Natural science
Athletic involvement	Who has access?	Predict performance?
Physical education curricula	Links with community?	Needs for healthy adults?
Daily exercise habits	Community resources?	Health outcome predictions?

America eventually became more firmly established as an academic discipline within the field of kinesiology.

That said, it is important to note foundational ties to the disciplines of sociology, history, philosophy, social psychology, anthropology, and economics. Sociology of sport and physical activity developed within a broader framework already established in kinesiology, and it has always been at the center of debates and goals in that field. The interdisciplinary structure of kinesiology has led to healthy arguments over the intellectual focus and worldview of the field, arguments that were at times framed by an early dualism of questions from the perspectives of sociology of sport and sport sociology. Sociology of sport includes sport as one component of the broader society, while a sport sociology poses questions about the social world and human interactions that emerge uniquely from sport settings (these questions had yet to be considered by most sociologists). This particular dualism proved false because the most promising analyses of sport and physical activity were clearly informed by both sociological inquiry and deep scholarly knowledge of human physical activity. Therefore, the field of sociology of sport, which is more deeply situated in kinesiology, also truly represents an intellectual collaboration of social scientists and physical educators that has taken place throughout historically and culturally crucial moments in human movement.

Pondering Play, Games, and Sport: 1800-1959

The development of areas of study or the disciplining of knowledge projects is a process unique to academic institutions and has been obvious throughout human history. Disciplines of study did not just appear along with the American university. In fact, famous philosophers such as Socrates, Plato, and Aristotle (each students of the other, respectively) were already considering and promoting varied categories of knowledge that would produce whole human beings, meaningful knowledge pursuits, and liberated lives. More recently, Immanuel Kant pondered what we can be "now," imagining that reality is a constant performance by each of us. The self-proclaimed father of sociology, Auguste Comte, promoted thinking about types of learning in which humans engaged. While the ideas of Kant and Comte may seem quite heady, each of these thinkers helped to usher in new ways of structuring how and what human beings ought to study and know in order to live a meaningful life. Like all modern-day academic areas of study, what began as merely a popular musing of what sport and physical activity had become following major societal changes, such as industrialization, technological advances, and a shift from rural to urban life, eventually led to ideas about a formal knowledge project or disciplined study.

TIMELINE

1800s

1839
First teacher training school opens in Massachusetts. The idea of physical education in schools takes hold.

1866
The state of California becomes the first to require physical education in school curriculum.

1896
Revival of Olympic Games in Athens, Greece.

1900-1959

1900
Most U.S. colleges and universities now have athletic associations and organized games and competitions.

1906
The Intercollegiate Athletic Association of the United States (IAAUS) is established and changes its name to the National Collegiate Athletic Association (NCAA) in 1910.

1916
Olympic Games are cancelled due to World War I.

1921
First NCAA Championships are offered (in the sport of track and field).

1924
First Winter Olympic Games are held.

1939
First NCAA basketball championship is held (the earliest version of "March Madness").

1940, 1944
Olympic Games are cancelled due to World War II.

(continued)

11

I'll tell you what I think of bicycling. . . I think it has done more to emancipate women than any one thing in the world.

Susan B. Anthony

Some of the first analyses of sport in society actually surfaced in the form of journalism and popular nonfiction writing. The turn of the 20th century was a turbulent, promising, confusing, exciting time for folks around the world, and sport and physical activity was one of the social settings that was changing along with other spheres of social life. Sport first appeared in popular print media regarding the culture of the day and in tomes meant to explain human behavior in a postindustrial world where people and their bodies had new relationships to work, leisure, technology, and style (see Boyle, 1963; Huizinga, 1949; Whyte, 1943/1955). For example, in an 1896 interview for *New York World*, human equality activist Susan B. Anthony was asked what she thought about the new trend in bicycling, especially among women. Anthony responded with this now-famous quote: "I'll tell you what I think of bicycling. . . I think it has done more to emancipate women than any one thing in the world" (Husted Harper, 1898, p. 859). In the mid-20th century, Boyle argued the following (1963, pp. 3-4):

> Sport is one of the major activities in American life today. Statistically, the figures are overwhelming. There are, for example, thirty million bowlers, sixteen million hunters, and six million golfers. . . . Sport permeates any number of levels of contemporary society, and it touches upon and even deeply influences such disparate elements as status, race relations, business life, automotive design, clothing styles, the concept of hero, language, and ethical values.

As well, prior to any imaginings of a field of study called sociology of sport and physical activity, there were anthropological analyses of games and play in "ethnic cultures," such as the ethnographic study of Balinese cock fighting in Indonesia (Geertz, 1973). As a result, this field that is now largely known as having had origins in academic workshops in Europe and North America actually had a much more full-bodied set of origins in the varied social spaces of sport. In fact, the pervasiveness of sport, physical activity, and new forms of leisure in a wildly changing postindustrial world became a concern for social scientists and led to early research and conceptual work that, intentional or not, would help to define and control social engagements with sport.

 ### Quick Facts

- Soccer, or association football, is played by 250 million people in more than 200 countries.
- Illinois is the only U.S. state to require daily physical education in K-12 schools.

CONCUSSIONS

In 1905, U.S. President Teddy Roosevelt, known as a rugged outdoorsman, convened a group of university presidents to discuss the dangers of college football. That year, several football players died as a result of their football injuries, and there was public outcry against the sport. In an effort to save the sport, Roosevelt met with the presidents to develop safety regulations. Out of those meetings came the creation of the National Collegiate Athletic Association (NCAA) to govern men's collegiate sport. Today, football faces a similar crisis with concussions. Former NFL All-Pro and Hall of Famer Junior Seau committed suicide and was found to have chronic traumatic encephalopathy. In 2013, the NFL settled a class action lawsuit, agreeing to pay over $700 million to the plaintiffs; however, the concussion issue remains one for all levels of football players, from Pop Warner to college to the NFL. Should we expect to see President Obama call a meeting of university presidents or NFL owners? Though the NFL is working to change their rules to enhance safety, many players and fans complain the new rules make the game soft. More than 100 years ago, college presidents convened to make college football safer. Today the NCAA seems more concerned with how to profit from the same players they claim to protect.

Defining the Field: 1960-1979

The early years in the development of the field we now call sociology of sport and physical activity was primarily focused on sport and had its intellectual origins in Europe and North America. Throughout this book, we rely on a social science definition of *sport* as more than an elite, competitive physical game. As noted earlier, the first known texts on sociology of sport were published in the 1920s, but it wasn't until the 1960s that a subdiscipline in the field of kinesiology began to take shape. Bringing sociology and physical education together in this enterprise, the International Committee for the Sociology of Sport (ICSS) was formed in 1964 and formally founded as a professional organization in 1965. By 1966, the first journal dedicated to sociological analyses of sport was launched, the *International Review for the Sociology of Sport* (IRSS), and 11 years later a second journal was initiated, the *Journal of Sport and Social Issues* (JSSI). A 1974 Commonwealth and International Conference symposium on the sociological study of sport led to the 1978 establishment of the North American Society for the Sociology of Sport (NASSS). NASSS held its first conference in 1980 in Denver, Colorado, and continues to be one of the key international organizations, along

epistemology—The study of knowledge: how it is developed, what it means, and what we imagine to be its purpose.

with ISSA, that facilitates ongoing scholarly meetings and peer-reviewed outlets for research in the field. With these significant building blocks in place, scholars continued to gather on an annual basis to advance theoretical and empirical work in the field.

This was a crucial time for identifying the aims of the field, connecting with relevant intellectual projects, and defining the field's object of analysis, key questions, and theoretical foci. These were no easy tasks for scholars in a fledgling field who sought to focus on an aspect of daily life that many viewed as fun and games or unimportant play time. In fact, even the field of sociology held an uneasy relationship with scholarly analyses of sport, ranking it 36th out of 37 subject areas in the American Sociological Association (Snyder & Spreitzer, 1979). Key debates included the everlasting sociological question of social structure versus culture as influences in human social interactions. **Epistemologies**, or ways of knowing and producing knowledge, were also in a process of establishment and revision in order to generate varied opportunities to produce new knowledge around cultural aspects of sport and physical activity. In 1969, John Loy and Gerald Kenyon asserted that they saw sport as a "unique discussion on the broad field of sociology for two specific reasons" (p. 2): the sheer magnitude of sport in society—it was omnipresent and hard to escape—and the potential for applying basic sociological theory to explain sporting spaces. In the same year, Loy and Kenyon attempted to advance the new field of study by making claims to do precisely what it was intending to accomplish. Accordingly, sport sociology would explain the following:

- The development of sport and physical activity
- Development as it occurs through sport and physical activity
- Human interaction in sport and physical activity
- The interrelationship between sport and other elements of culture

Moreover, the new field would be defined in this way (Loy & Kenyon, 1969, p. 83):

> The sociology of sport in its broadest sense is concerned with the description and explanation of the interrelationships between sport and various levels of society. . . . More specifically, sport sociology is the study of primary units of social life, basic social institutions, and fundamental social processes influencing and affected by human behavior in sport situations. The distinguishing feature of a sociological approach to the analyses of sport in contrast to other approaches long employed is its focus upon social organization.

Proponents of the new field of study were well aware that their knowledge project would be different from those of the natural sciences in kinesiology, and so statements about the role of the sport sociologist expressed a desire for a "value-free" science (Kenyon & Loy, 1965, p. 25):

> The sport sociologist does not base his inquiries upon the assumption that "physical activity is good." Sport sociology as we view it, is a value-free social science. It is not an effort to influence public opinion or behavior, nor is it an attempt to find support for the "social development" objective of physical education. . . . The sport sociologist is neither the spreader of the gospel nor an evangelist for exercise. His function is not to shape attitudes and values but rather to describe and explain them.

These proclamations were attempts to situate the new field of study as one of rigor and significance in the realm of studies of the social world.

It is not that these early scholars were not also fans of sport, but they saw themselves as architects of a field of study that would be seen either as an extension of other rigorous science or potentially as a space for "cheerful robots" invested in sport, as Mills (1959/2004) argued. He believed that if we do not develop the skills for seeing our social world through a sociological imagination, we will merely mechanistically (or mechanically?) go along with any societal trend that promises to make our personal lives better. In line with Mills, the early architects of the sociology of sport and physical activity endeavored to invite a purposeful analysis of the role of human physical activity and sporting spaces in everyday life.

By the 1970s, more than 30 colleges and universities offered courses featuring the role of sport in society, and there were at least three doctoral programs for studying the sociology of sport

 DR. HARRY EDWARDS, SCHOLAR-ACTIVIST

Harry Edwards wrote the first textbook in the field of sport sociology in 1973, *Sociology of Sport*. He received his PhD in sociology at Cornell University and spent his academic career teaching at the University of California at Berkeley. His seminal work, *The Revolt of the Black Athlete*, published in 1969, identified the relationships between race, sport, and politics. It was one of the first publications to acknowledge racism in American sport. His 1973 textbook was pub-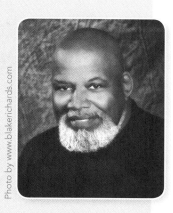
lished years before the organization of the North American Society for the Sociology of Sport, and it provided the basis for subsequent scholarly investigations of the topic. In addition to his work as a faculty member, Dr. Edwards was instrumental in the Olympic Project for Human Rights, a social justice movement that gained international recognition during the 1968 Summer Games in Mexico City. Dr. Edwards also served as an advisor to the San Francisco 49ers football and the Golden State Warriors basketball teams and served his local community when he was named the director of parks and recreation in Oakland, California, a position he held until 2003.

Photo by www.blakerichards.com

1960-1979
(continued)

1972
Title IX is passed into law, signed by President Richard M. Nixon.

1973
The book *Definitions and Clarifications in Sociology of Sport* by Harry Edwards is published by Dorsey Press.

1977
The first issue of the *Journal of Sport and Social Issues* is published.

1978
North American Society for the Sociology of Sport is established.

1980-1999

1980
First conference of the North American Society for the Sociology of Sport is held in Denver, Colorado.

1984
The *Sociology of Sport Journal* is launched, becoming the official journal of the North American Society for the Sociology of Sport.

1993
The ICSS changes its name to the International Sport Sociology Association (ISSA).

2000-2015

2011
World Congress of Sociology of Sport, "Sport and the Winds of Change," is held in Havana, Cuba.

2015
The 50th anniversary of ISSA is celebrated in Paris, France.

(Loy & Kenyon, 1969). At this point, scholarly research areas included sport and socialization; sport and social stratification in and through sport; deviance in sporting contexts; sport and violence; sport, politics, and nationalism; mass-mediated sport; embodiment; and particular sporting communities (e.g., Major League Baseball [MLB] wives, alternative sport athletes).

A Maturing, Multidisciplinary Field: 1980 to 1999

Given the building blocks of the first 20 years of the field, scholars were now ready to move in new directions and dig for deeper understandings of sport and physical activity in society. As an example, rather than asking if social inequalities were also relevant in sport settings, new questions focused on how social inequalities took shape in varied sporting contexts. Scholars developed an increasingly nuanced understanding of sport involvement; identities in sport settings; social hierarchies in sport; and sport as an economic, political, and mediated aspect of culture.

In 1984, the *Sociology of Sport Journal* would become yet another outlet for research in the field. Emerging topics at this time included sport and nationalism, globalization, body size, disability studies, wellness, and medicalization of bodies. Postmodern theorizing and cultural studies analyses were also becoming increasingly common and useful in the sociology of sport and physical activity. These theoretical approaches offered new ways to study and understand the deep, diverse meanings that human physical activity may have for people in various contexts, conditions, and geographic locations.

 REACTIONS TO *MEAT ON THE HOOF*

In 1972, Gary Shaw published *Meat on the Hoof: The Hidden World of Texas Football*, exposing the underworld of college football. Shaw revealed the method that Coach Darrell Royal used to get the most out of his football players at the University of Texas. Shaw was a reserve player at Texas from 1963 to 1967. At the time, the gritty details troubled many sport fans and critics alike, though there was also outcry against Shaw for exposing the secrets of college football. His book detailed hazing rituals, abuse by coaches, recruiting practices, and general abuse of nonstarters. Shaw's tell-all was among the first of several books by elite athletes to expose the locker room culture to the American public. Pitcher Jim Bouton published his tell-all, *Ball Four*, in 1970, detailing his season with the Seattle Pilots.

1. Why do you think readers responded as they did to Shaw's revelations?

2. What sort of reactions might we expect today if a tell-all locker room book were published?

3. What changes in culture have occurred that might explain the shift (or lack of shift) in responses?

4. Why are locker rooms and team cultures such secret celebrated spaces?

One of the major contributions at this time was an emerging methodology for understanding sport as a space where hierarchies or difference play out, especially in subtle ways. Not all examples of racism in sport, for example, are explicit exclusions followed by enlightened inclusions, like the typical recollection of Jackie Robinson's entry to Major League Baseball. In this intellectual moment, sociologists of sport and physical activity were gaining intellectual ground in the unveiling of subtle racially coded (or gendered, or sexualized, or classed) messages that were reinforced through sport, like beliefs that Latinos were great baseball athletes but not necessarily good candidates for team managers and coaches, or that Latinos from outside the United States had a special hunger for the rewards that a professional baseball career might offer (González, 1996; Regalado, 1998).

These types of everyday experiences of social categorization and power are not easily understood through classical sociological theories, although aspects of this sort of inequality are observable through classical and critical theories. It is through this postmodern and cultural studies sensemaking of everyday investments in ideas about race, social class, gender, and sexuality that sport and physical activity came into view as spaces for both liberation and containment of human difference.

Current Status of the Field: The New Millennium, 2000-2015

By now, it should be clear that sociologists of sport and physical activity analyze the social arrangements and shared beliefs that underlie physical activity. Although the sociology of sport and physical activity has largely focused on sport, the field has expanded to include analyses of exercise, public health, conceptions of the body, and physical education. To be sure, today's cadre of sociologists of sport and physical activity pose valuable questions about a wide array of sporting, schooling, and exercising spaces. Accordingly, the most recent decade in the field has produced new knowledge about global sport, exercise communities like CrossFit and Tough Mudder competitions, alternative and lifestyle sports, fan communities, online gaming, coaching, and medicalization of physical activity.

Sociological analyses of sport and physical activity are well established beyond the United States, including Asia and growing scholarly enclaves in South America and Africa. While the field began as an international scholarly conversation of sorts, it was initially informed by North America and Western Europe. An increasingly global application of the sociological imagination will surely help make sense of social problems within and beyond sport and will offer opportunities to understand the ways that sport and physical activity illuminate current social conditions.

Today, sociologists of sport and physical activity primarily work in three major categories: descriptive sociology, analytic sociology, and applied sociology. Within each of these categories of knowledge production, social scientists most often analyze sport settings, but they also study physical education and exercise settings (see figure 1.1).

You will see these categories of analysis throughout the text, and they are meant to allow us to have a more comprehensive understanding of the depth of sociological analyses. These categories are not discrete—there is considerable overlap—but they are useful for articulating the developing foci in the field and the varied manner in

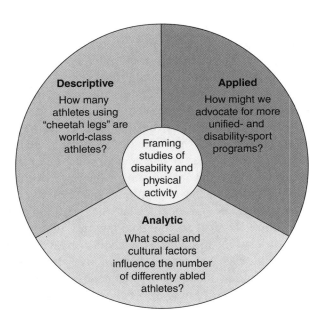

FIGURE 1.1   Sociology at work.

which intellectual projects may be pursued. As you may already realize, it would be easy to focus all of our attention on organized, elite sport, but it is timely and relevant to consider the embodied experiences of members of society in the three cultural spaces of sport, physical education, and exercise.

Functions of Sociology of Sport and Physical Activity

Sociologists of sport and physical activity most often work as faculty members in colleges or universities, but some have put their skills to use in sports journalism, research centers, public policy, and sport management. Courses taught by sociologists of sport include Sport in Society; Sport, Gender, and Media; Sport and Social Inequalities; Global Relations in Sporting Contexts; Sport and Feminisms; Postcolonial Bodies; Physical Cultural Studies in Human Movement; Sport in Cinematic Representation, and Queer Sport Studies (Longest, 2008).

Recall that by the early 1970s, it was estimated that 30 (roughly less than 1%) U.S. institutions of higher education offered a course focusing on the role of sport in society, and three universities offered doctoral programs in the sociology of sport (Loy & Kenyon, 1969). A 1984 survey of members of the NASSS found that 69 percent of the members' home institutions offered an undergraduate course in sport sociology (Brooks, 1984). More recently, Nixon (2010) found that half of

U.S. institutions offered one or more undergraduate sport sociology courses, with the majority of courses offered through departments of kinesiology rather than sociology. Also of interest was the fact that 86 percent of these courses focused their content knowledge on sport, 57 percent of courses were organized in ways that utilized more than one discipline for content knowledge (multidisciplinary), and 44 percent had a sociological focus.

These last data points indicate that as an undergraduate student, you are most likely to find an intellectually integrated course in the sociology of sport and physical activity offered by your department of kinesiology. Most of these courses will focus on sport, not physical education or exercise, and information and ideas will be presented from various disciplines, such as history, sociology, anthropology, and cultural studies. The number of social science courses offered and the interdisciplinary nature of these courses reflect a period of growth for the field of study, a growth that has more recently slowed.

At the graduate level of study, there are currently 840 U.S. institutions granting degrees in kinesiology; among these are 61 doctoral granting institutions, and among those, 11 clearly offer doctoral study in sociological analyses of sport (Thomas, 2008; see list in appendix A). One estimate in the early 1980s reported approximately 100 practicing sociology of sport scholars around the world (Luschen & Sage, 1981). Today, there are at least 400 as indicated by membership in professional organizations. The elements of preparing for a career in sociology of sport and physical activity are more specifically outlined in chapter 2, but as a preview, here is one example of a scholar in sociology of sport and physical activity.

 ## DR. RICHARD LAPCHICK, INSTITUTE FOR DIVERSITY AND ETHICS IN SPORT

The Institute for Diversity and Ethics in Sport (TIDES) was founded in 2002 by Dr. Richard Lapchick and the DeVos Sport Business Management graduate program at the University of Central Florida. TIDES examines issues related to gender and race in intercollegiate and professional sport and publishes annual reports assessing student-athlete graduation rates, as well as hiring practices in sport, in their Race and Gender Report Card series.

Dr. Richard Lapchick received his PhD in the field of international race relations at the University of Denver. Lapchick founded the Center for the Study of Sport in Society at Northeastern University in Boston in 1984 and serves as the director emeritus. He is also the president of the National Consortium for Academics and Sports. Lapchick led the sports boycott against South Africa from 1975 until the end of apartheid.

Photo courtesy Robert Weathers of University of Central Florida.

Goals of the Field

In a nutshell, sociologists of sport and physical activity investigate human physical activity as it relates to changing social conditions, patterns of access, and relations of power with an intention to enhance people's lives by thoughtfully advocating for a humane, physically active society. People who work in sport and physical activity and view it through a sociological lens typically advocate the following goals:

- To understand the societal values, beliefs, and structures that undergird sport and physical activity
- To advocate for societal-level support of diverse forms of sport and physical activity, including play, organized leisure, instructional activity, and elite competition
- To identify and address inequalities and unfair social arrangements within sport and physical activity contexts
- To advance an imagination of a global society where human physical activity is celebrated, resourced, and liberated rather than exploited, commodified, and regulated
- To collaborate with sport and physical activity leaders toward the common goal of creating a humane, physically active society

To be clear, the stakeholders in this set of goals are not merely the academic social scientists and sport policy makers but also you, the everyday citizen who has an

 EXPANDING YOUR ORIGIN STORIES

Consider all the aspects of your multiple identities and how they intersect. Some of these identities are your gender, race or ethnicity, able-bodiedness or disability, religion, nationality, and geographic region.

1. How do these factors influence your decisions?
   a. Whether to participate (or not) in certain sports and physical activities
   b. Whether to become a fan of certain sports or teams
   c. How you adorn your body for physical activity and sport
   d. How you view issues related to sport and physical activity, like performance-enhancing drugs (PEDs), government subsidies to professional sport teams for stadium financing, obesity rates, CrossFit, and the Olympics, to name a few
2. Can you begin to see the ways your multiple identities intersect with one another (and how difficult it is to just see yourself as one singular identity)?

interest in a life that includes accessible, meaningful physical activity throughout your lifetime. The tools of sociology of sport and physical activity may be put to use for the common good by neighbors who wish to create a safe space for outdoor play, school community members who desire a high-quality physical education program in their public school system, fans of professional sports who want to see more equity in men's and women's professional sport opportunities, and athletes who want increasingly fair labor practices for themselves and their colleagues.

The Short of It

- Understanding sport as more than physical—as also cultural—is a requirement for anyone interested in applying a sociological analysis to human movement.
- Sociological analysis emerged as a crucial sphere of kinesiology (previously known as physical education) in the 1960s, but it also reflects an intellectual collaboration of social scientists and physical educators throughout historically and culturally crucial moments in human movement.
- The International Committee for the Sociology of Sport (ICSS) was formed in 1964 and formally founded as a professional organization in 1965. By 1966, the first journal dedicated to sociological analysis of sport was launched, the *International Review for the Sociology of Sport (IRSS)*.
- Sociology of sport is the study of primary units of social life, basic social institutions, and fundamental social processes influencing and affected by human behavior in sport situations.
- Sociologists of sport and physical activity most often work as faculty members in colleges or universities, but some have put their skills to use in sport journalism, research centers, public policy, and sport management.

CHAPTER 2

What Can I Do With Sociology of Sport and Physical Activity?

In this chapter you will learn the following:

✓ Professional application of sociological knowledge in sport and physical activity

✓ Requirements for professional practices in these varied roles

✓ Work activities within these different roles

✓ Contributions made by professionals in these roles

✓ Ways sociological knowledge can be applied beyond professional roles

> It is clear that many performance and wellness issues stem from facets of life that influence both the physical and social-cultural aspects of the body.
>
> **Keri Flynn**, athletic trainer
> (Duncan & Jamieson, 2012)

What in the world will you do with formal knowledge in sociology, let alone sociology of sport and physical activity? How might you develop this knowledge? How long will it take to develop an appropriate amount of knowledge and experience? How will you put this knowledge to use? These are common questions about any focused project in knowledge acquisition, but these are especially relevant to humanities-focused forms of knowledge today. The **humanities** (or the classical fields of study like history, sociology, philosophy, and anthropology) are highly valued but are less obviously linked to paid labor positions, also known as jobs. The goal of this chapter is to help you understand that you needn't work as a sociologist of sport in order to find social science knowledge useful in everyday life.

Consider a trip to a foreign country. Part of the excitement is experiencing something new and challenging yourself to experience a new language, customs, and foods. You do not need to become a citizen of that country in order to learn how to observe local customs and ways of life. You might consult a guidebook or a translation dictionary of common phrases, or you may even talk with friends who have traveled to this place or any other place away from home. You will want to know the major structures and resources of the place you will visit, such as transportation systems, holidays, sacred sites, unique local products if you like to shop, and gendered, religious, and cultural customs. If you have already traveled to a foreign country, it is likely that this experience led you to think in new ways about your home country. This is how a sociological lens and sociocultural knowledge are relevant—it is like an intentional travel journal or a guidebook for life experiences, a way to open your eyes to the vast examples of human social interaction that unfold in your everyday social settings. Toward this end, sociologists of sport and physical activity work in varied ways to offer crucial insight into the way the social world is structured and the kinds of human interactions that take place in sport and physical activity settings.

The beauty of a sociological perspective is that it can be applied in everyday spaces. Recall that a sociological perspective requires the willingness and ability to look beyond our personal experiences and see patterns in the social world, expectations or norms, actions, and context or conditions. Your development of sociological skills and knowledge around sport and physical activity may inform your work as a physical educator, leisure professional, athletic trainer, or coach, and it will likely also inform your own political activism as a citizen who values meaningful physical activity for all members of society.

humanities—The study of humans' processing and documenting their social worlds, typically expressed through religion, philosophy, literature, art, music, dance or ritual movement, history, and language.

This chapter invites you to explore the many ways that you can apply your developing knowledge of sociology of sport and physical activity. The description of opportunities is somewhat artificially split by advocacy, allied professional practice, and academic professional practice. While it is important to understand the types of preparation required for performing different forms of personal and professional work within the sociology of sport and physical activity, try not to get bogged down with boundaries between these applied practices. The crucial point here is that skills and knowledge in the sociology of sport and physical activity ought to be developed and applied in a number of social contexts with as much cross-disciplinary collaboration as possible. As people and professionals who are linked through a value for lifelong physical activity, we do our best work when we are able to collectively imagine, investigate, and advance a society with commitment to meaningful physical activity for all communities and members of society.

Stakeholders and Professionals in Sociology of Sport and Exercise

- Advocates for ethical and humane sport and physical activity
  - Athletes and participants
  - Parents
  - Volunteer coaches
  - Community sport leaders
- Allied professionals in sport and physical activity
  - Directors of community sport programs
  - Sport advocacy networks
  - Sport- and health-focused journalists
  - Active leisure tour directors
  - Worksite wellness coordinators
  - Coaches, physical educators, fitness leaders, physical therapists, and athletic trainers
- Academic professionals
  - Full-time professors in departments of kinesiology or sociology
  - Part-time instructors in departments of kinesiology or sociology
  - Directors of research centers
  - Directors of sport policy institutes

Advocates for Ethical and Humane Sports and Physical Activity

Some of the most powerful people in everyday aspects of sport and physical activity are parents in youth program settings, volunteer coaches, and community members who use their social roles to advance preferred forms of sport for participants, teams, and neighborhoods (e.g., national movement for open streets). The required skills in this category of applied practice are not formally sanctioned, but any ethical advocacy for sport and physical activity that advances a preferred society would include at least the following:

- Study of local policy, access, and leadership issues
- Voluntary study of social movements and social science perspectives
- Willingness to ask difficult questions about valued spaces for sport and physical activity
- Willingness to partner with others in advancing sport and physical activity
- Completion of specific program or organization training such as increasingly required training for parents of participants in community youth sport programs

Recall the example from chapter 1 of Nancy Lopez, who had to go before the school board to gain a spot on her high school golf team. This is an example of advocacy for ethical and humane sport and physical activity.

Regardless of one's relation to the allied professionals or academic professionals, the duties of advocates apply to all who care to fully engage their role as active members of their communities. Duties for this group are not sanctioned or governed by any overarching agency, but actually exist in more of a social contract, or a collective civil and civic engagement in one's school, neighborhood, club, hometown, team, state, or country. We can consider the ongoing duty from three angles:

- Application of a sociological lens to identify meaningful social issues and projects in relation to sport and physical activity
- Willingness to organize a project for addressing social issues through sport and physical activity
- Ability to support and promote projects that increase the capacity of communities to have accessible daily physical activity outlets for all members of society

 Quick Fact

Fifty percent of participants in Open Streets and Cyclovia events report increased physical activity as a result. Many become advocates for safer bicycling communities, and some discover new resources in their own communities.

As one example, a local bike shop owner organizes beginner rides and partners with a community group that develops bike lanes and aims to decrease the town's reliance on automobiles. Yes, the bike shop owner wants to sell bicycles, but she also sees bicycles as part of a larger issue regarding community health and a national reliance on gasoline-fueled transportation. This citizen is going beyond selling bikes as she engages in creating a community where daily bicycling can be an easy, safe, and accessible choice for all members.

In contrast, consider the agitative politically focused bicycle activism of Critical Mass bike rides. Rather than bringing people together solely for a leisurely physical activity, Critical Mass bike rides intentionally take over major auto thoroughfares and draw attention to global reliance on oil and automobiles. In a Critical Mass bike ride, the bicycle and its riders become social activists, or community change agents. These divergent examples of bicycling show that everyday physical activity can have a significant effect on community members and social structures.

Allied Professionals in the Sociology of Sport and Physical Activity

In the current moment, perhaps the most prominent allied professions in the field of sociology of sport and physical activity are directors of community sport programs, sport advocacy networks, sport-focused journalists, active leisure tour directors, and worksite wellness coordinators. These allied professionals are included here due to the magnitude of their engagement with the citizenry—they interact with a number of people every day. Although allied professionals do not specialize in sociological analyses of sport and physical activity, they typically have a complementary social science background that supports their applied work in sport and social issues.

Allied professionals will likely have met particular professional standards in another field and completed at least three postsecondary courses in social science methodologies and social and behavioral sciences related to sport and physical activity. These courses typically include current scholarly knowledge in serving special populations, planning programs, identifying program needs, assessment of outcome goals, and program management. High-quality professional programs of study also require some sort of field experience where students demonstrate an ability to apply

 It took countless hours on and off the field to recognize that each athlete has their own story to tell, and being willing to hear it has allowed me to establish a professional camaraderie built on trust that is the key to success in my career.

Keri Flynn, athletic trainer (Duncan & Jamieson, 2012)

not only their specialized skills and knowledge but also their content-related skills and knowledge. Students working in worksite wellness will demonstrate core abilities to plan wellness programs as well as the ability to assess the social conditions and context in which they implement those programs. Moreover, an allied professional will be able to determine when the social conditions and context require additional insight and thus will consult a colleague from the scholarly profession. Most students who earn a bachelor's degree in the field of kinesiology will cultivate a background in sociocultural analyses and will be able to apply this along with other scientific knowledge in their everyday professional practice.

Allied professionals may apply the sociological lens much as advocates do—as a thread that is continuously woven throughout their imagining of and engagement in sport and physical activity programs. A major difference between allied professionals and advocates, however, is the context of professional practice.

For allied professionals, their application of the sociological lens must be somehow intertwined with their overarching professional goals, which may be quite varied. Someone who runs a yoga studio and observes that the studio is serving only adult women with upper income levels may see this as an opportunity to alter the fee scale, expand the types of classes offered, or change the schedule of classes to invite a more diverse group of community members into the practice of yoga. Likewise, a tennis instructor may find that her students come from only one end of town, which may prompt her to advocate for more public tennis courts in all neigh-

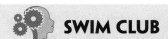 **SWIM CLUB**

DeLuca (2013) examined the privileged space of a swim club. Based on four years of ethnographic data, DeLuca concluded that swim clubs maintain a White upper-class space of privilege. As a swimming coach at the Pine View Swim and Tennis Club, De Luca took extensive ethnographic field notes over the course of four years and conducted 35 interviews with mothers and swimmers. She found that swimming pools serve as community centers that reinforce community identity and membership, provide social networking for children and their parents, and represent a segregated social space. Pine View is a White homogenous space. Through interviews and observations, DeLuca concluded that the members of Pine View were able to maintain a segregated space reserved for White upper-class members. Belonging to the club and pool "was an exercise in the acquisition, transmission, and reproduction of specific class-based capitals as in swimming" (p. 359).

1. How might DeLuca's findings illustrate the overlapping roles of advocates, allied professionals, and academic professionals ?

2. Would her results have been different if she had observed a different sport setting, specifically one that had a different racial and socioeconomic class population?

borhoods and to offer beginner clinics in neighborhoods where involvement is low. At a more elite level, a professional athlete may partner with his sport organization to bring attention to social problems, as was the case of Cathy Freeman and the Australian nation addressing rights of Aboriginal people and their presence in the 2000 Sydney Summer Olympic Games.

In summary, allied professionals may engage their sociological lens to enhance sport and physical activity every day in their professional practice: This happens every time they refuse to treat a female athlete like a "girl" and instead treat her like an athlete, or organize a sport program that is open to all community members regardless of ability, or write a letter to the school board outlining the community benefits of high-quality physical education programs.

 # DR. DEANNE BROOKS, ASSISTANT PROFESSOR, SALEM COLLEGE

DeAnne Brooks is an assistant professor of exercise science at Salem College. She holds degrees in kinesiology and clinical exercise physiology. She is a certified strength and conditioning specialist and certified exercise physiologist and has 16 years of experience coaching track at the youth, high school, and collegiate levels. The sociological imagination has been important to Brooks in her work to promote and provide opportunities for members of all groups to participate in sports and health-related physical activity. For example, in her coaching role at the American Hebrew Academy, Brooks has observed that most high school track and field championships take place on Fridays and Saturdays, presumably because these days allow for minimal interference with school and the Christian Sabbath (Sunday; the Jewish Sabbath is on Friday and Saturday). Brooks sees this practice as a religious hierarchy that privileges the Christian majority and marginalizes religious minorities whose traditions and beliefs operate in conflict with established, dominant norms. She has worked with rules and planning committees to organize track and field championships in ways that are reflective of various religious traditions, making participation possible for the Jewish athletes she coaches.

As a personal trainer in cardiac facilities and corporate fitness centers, Brooks noticed that members of racial minority and lower socioeconomic groups were underrepresented in these programs. She has researched ways to make health-related physical activity programs accessible, attractive, and welcoming to members of underrepresented groups, such as offering a convenient physical activity program for parents during their children's team practice sessions. Through these allied professional activities, Dr. Brooks is contributing to the creation of a more physically active society.

Academic Professionals in the Sociology of Sport and Physical Activity

Sociologists of sport and physical activity most often work as faculty members in colleges or universities, but some have put their skills to use in research centers, public policy, and sport management. Faculty who primarily focus on sociological analysis of sport and physical activity in their scholarly work have typically completed doctoral degrees in kinesiology or sociology.

The majority of academic jobs that focus on sociocultural analyses of sport and physical activity are located in departments of kinesiology, and so an academic background in kinesiology is expected at some point in one's academic studies. For example, one may complete an undergraduate degree in kinesiology (perhaps including an advanced-placement high school course in sociocultural analyses of sport) or sociology, followed by a master's degree in either field, and then a doctoral degree involving some sort of sociological or cultural studies analysis of sport and physical activity.

While most students on this path complete doctoral degrees in kinesiology with an emphasis in sociological analyses, some programs of study in sociology, American studies, and cultural studies also focus on sport, the body, health, and leisure. Given these three degree strands, students on this path are likely to spend at least 10 years in academic study beyond high school in order to prepare for a career as an academic professional in the sociology of sport and physical activity.

Graduate coursework includes intensive study in a variety of social science perspectives as applied to sport and physical activity (see figure 2.1).

Building on the abbreviated descriptions of key professionals from chapter 1, let's take a look at the specific duties of different types of professionals in the academic field of sociology of sport and physical activity. Typically, those who earn a doctoral degree in this field put it to use as a full-time faculty member at a college or university. In this role, the main responsibilities are most often teaching and conducting research. Of course these assignments have some variability, with some folks teaching more and others spending more time on research endeavors. Teaching usually includes courses for both undergraduate and graduate students with the content focus gaining in depth and specificity as students move toward the upper division of graduate coursework. As mentioned previously, courses taught by sociologists of sport typically include Sport in Society; Sport, Gender, and Media; Sport and Social Inequalities; Global Relations in Sporting Contexts; Sport and Feminisms; Postcolonial Bodies; Physical Cultural Studies in Human Movement; Sport in Cinematic Representation; and Queer Sport Studies (Longest, 2008). Most instructors of courses in sociology of sport and physical activity hold positions in departments of kinesiology and focus their courses on sport, but a growing number also pay close attention to physical activity and health.

FIGURE 2.1 Sample doctoral degree in sociology of sport and physical activity.

Fall Semester (9)

KIN630: Race, Class, Gender, Sport (3)

Non-KIN core (SOC, HIS, CUL, WGS)

KIN: Behavioral studies course (3)

Fall Semester (9)

Non-KIN core (SOC, HIS, CUL, WGS)

KIN614: Qualitative Inquiry in HHP (3)

Non-KIN core (SOC, HIS, CUL, WGS)

Fall Semester (9)

KIN710: Sport and Feminisms (3)

Research course (3)

Independent study (3)

Fall Semester (6)

Dissertation hours (6)

Spring Semester (9)

KIN632: Global and Ethnic Relations (3)

KIN 610: Research Methods (3)

Non-KIN core (SOC, HIS, CUL, WGS)

Spring Semester (9)

KIN635: Gender-Sport Psych (3)

KIN644: Psych of Sport and Exercise (3)

Research course (3)

Spring Semester (9)

KIN elective (3)

Dissertation hours (6)

Additional requirements

Minimum total hours = 60; minimum total KIN hours = 30

Key: KIN: kinesiology; HIS: history; SOC: sociology; CUL: Cultural Studies; WGS: Women's and Gender Studies.

Some academic professionals mix their faculty roles with leadership in research centers. For example, Dr. Richard Lapchick is the director of the Institute for Diversity and Ethics in Sport (TIDES) at the University of Central Florida, and Dr. Mary Jo Kane was the director of the Tucker Center for Research on Girls and Women in Sport at the University of Minnesota. In setting up and leading major research centers, these faculty members are actively developing new knowledge in the field while simultaneously preparing young professionals in research skills. Social scientists in research centers use a variety of research methodologies, often including data on rates of participation, access to resources, cultural meanings of sporting events and moments, and outcomes of policies around equity, especially in sport and schooling settings. Despite the range of approaches to research, producing new sociological knowledge in a trustworthy manner is a crucial aspect of the academic work of professionals in this field of study.

⭐ DR. MARY JO KANE, TUCKER CENTER FOR RESEARCH ON GIRLS AND WOMEN IN SPORT

Photo courtesy of University of Minnesota

The Tucker Center is an interdisciplinary research center that examines the role and influence of sport and physical activity on the lives of girls and women. Founded in 1993 by University of Minnesota faculty Dr. Dorothy McNeill Tucker and Dr. Mary Jo Kane, the center has three goals: collaborative research, research that counts, and education. The Tucker Center has produced one video documentary, *Concussions and Female Athletes: The Untold Story*. In 2007 it published the report "Developing Physically Active Girls: An Evidence-Based Multidisciplinary Approach." In addition, the Tucker Center has current projects examining media representations of female athletes and female coaches, youth sport, Title IX, and female coaches.

Dr. Kane received her PhD from the University of Illinois in sport sociology and currently is the director of the Tucker Center. She also holds the Dorothy McNeill and Elbridge Ashcraft Tucker Chair for Women in Exercise Science and Sport, the first endowed chair related to women and sport.

Building New Sociological Knowledge in Sport and Physical Activity

Noted sociologist D. Stanley Eitzen described the challenging perspective that each of our highlighted practitioners choose to apply in their professional practice (2002, p. 8):

> I emphasize the negative aspects of sport in order to demythologize and demystify it. Yet, I do not want to forget the magical nature of sport that is so captivating and compelling. Overcoming this basic contradiction—being critical of sport while retaining a love for it—will enable us to improve this vital, interesting, and exciting aspect of social life.

He went on to list a number of paradoxes of sport, or contradictory realities of sport settings. For example, as chapter 6 discusses, sport is both unifying and divisive for nations and other communities. As well, when describing diversity and difference, chapter 5 talks about the contradictory ways that sport is both inclusive and exclusive. Sociologists of sport and physical activity endeavor to unveil the ways that sport reflects a range of conditions that exist in society.

This work is undertaken not to undermine sport or physical activity, but as Eitzen (2002) argued, to enable us to enhance this crucial, provocative, and exciting aspect of social life and human interaction. Social scientists who are not also trained in kinesiology sometimes minimize the cultural importance of sport, physical activity, and the body. Kinesiologists with no humanities training often value the cultural aspects of physicality less than performance issues. A person with interest and knowledge in both how human beings move and what this movement means in different moments and under changing social conditions can bridge these divides and imagine a society where all members are meaningfully engaged in physical activity throughout their lives.

Applying a critical perspective to something you enjoy and value is not an easy task, yet as Dr. Eitzen (2002) so eloquently stated, it is a necessary task in order to enhance sport and maintain its vitality in everyday social life. This is especially true for academic professionals, who are typically expected to conduct research and create new, meaningful knowledge about the social needs and benefits related to sport and physical activity. In order to advance this important work, sociologists of sport and physical activity use a variety of scientific tools, analytic strategies, and communication techniques. The most prominent scientific tools for social scientists are theories or tested explanations about the way society functions.

 **CROSSFIT**

CrossFit is a strength and conditioning program developed by Greg Glassman in 2000. The fitness regimen is based on high-intensity workouts using body-weight exercises and movements with weights. A CrossFit culture has emerged due to the strong element of camaraderie and competition among its participants. The CrossFit Games began in 2007 with male and female competitions in various age divisions. CrossFit offers certifications and franchises, and allows use of the CrossFit name only with such certifications. CrossFit has enjoyed a surge in popularity, and there are now 7,000 CrossFit gyms in the United States. Recent critiques of CrossFit have focused on the rate of injuries among participants. Some argue that the movements in CrossFit aren't new or innovative but are marketed as a new way to achieve fitness goals.

CrossFit involves a lot of high-intensity training but can also foster fun competition among its participants.

structural (macro) theories— Social science explanations featuring the major components of society and their effect on everyday life experiences.

cultural (micro) theories—Social science explanations featuring human interaction and meaning making in particular social sites, such as family settings, friendship groups, or sport teams.

interactionist theory—Social science explanations featuring the day-to-day interaction between people and social structures, such as your experience as a student in the American educational system.

landscape—Broad social conditions, such as national and global surveys and census data sets.

experience—An understanding that emerges from firsthand observation or participation in a particular social space.

analytic knowledge—Knowledge focused on ways of understanding and making sense of daily interactions in the social world.

General theories in sociology of sport are informed by classical and contemporary theorizing in the so-called parent disciplines of sociology, anthropology, history, and cultural studies, and may be categorized by their main focus or defining parameters. Some theories focus on how entire social systems operate, including what counts as their major components (e.g., families, economy, education, religion, or politics) and try to explain these systems and the role of sport within them as either harmonious or inherently unequal in structure. Not surprisingly, given their focus on major components of societal structures, the aforementioned theories are called **structural theories** (sometimes referred to as **macro theories**). Other theoretical perspectives attempt to explain the core values and collective meanings assigned to human interactions, including those that occur in sport and physical activity. These are broadly referred to as **cultural theories**. They reflect **micro theoretical perspectives**, or those that focus on more local subcultural contexts, like a team or a club. As mentioned in chapter 1, sociologists are always concerned with both structure and culture. As a result, some begin their studies of sport and physical activity from what is called an **interactionist** theoretical perspective, or one that attempts to identify and explain the complex interaction between the self and society. For example, an interactionist perspective may seek to explain the external influence of sport team membership on students' sense of status in their school community.

Analytic strategies and research techniques for sociological analyses are also quite varied, and are often related to the theoretical tools mentioned previously. In general, sociologists engage in what we call *landscape*, *experience*, and *analytic knowledge* techniques. When you read big data tables that describe rates of participation in particular sports and physical activities, you are reading social demography, or data that help to explain the sport and physical activity **landscape**.

You may have participated in the U.S. Census survey, which is one example of a study in social demography or an attempt to count people, living arrangements, income levels, and leisure-time activities in order to get a large-scale glimpse of American life. Similarly, in examining gender in the Olympic and Paralympic Games, Smith and Wrynn (2010, 2013) tallied the number of female and male athletes in each Olympic and Paralympic sport to determine which sports and which national Olympic and Paralympic committees were more and less gender equitable. They collected their data from the results of the actual events, not by talking to athletes.

Landscape data are very informative, but they do not explain all there is to know about a society or even a community. So, we move on to more in-depth and localized techniques of research, or techniques that underscore everyday lived **experience**. In this sort of research, sociologists of sport and physical activity may actually talk with and observe people in real sport and physical activity settings and then make some assertions about the role or importance of that particular physical activity setting in the lives of those particular people.

Analytic knowledge techniques would privilege the application of theory to explain the meaning, influence, and use of sport or physical activity in both localized and collective (societal) contexts. For example, Catherine Palmer (2001) studied the Tour de France bike race in order to better understand international and global relations around French politics and identities. Palmer, also a cyclist, traveled with a team and conducted observations and interviews as she journeyed through French, Spanish, and Basque communities. Through these conversations and field observations, she was able to understand the ways that this bike race was also a significant marker of national identity in different ways for different communities. The analytic technique places sport and physical activity into a broader perspective on cultural context and human interactions—it is not so much about the sport activity but about the human interactions that occur as part of the sporting space.

The third aspect of this research process for sociologists of sport and physical activity is communication of their ideas and analyses. Academic professionals share the majority of the research they conduct with other academics through professional journals, books, and conference presentations. Many scholars also attempt to collaborate on projects and share their findings with community groups (e.g., Girl Scouts, neighborhood associations, and schools) and practitioners (e.g., physical educators, program leaders, or exercise professionals). Through these sorts of collaborations, academic professionals can share their ideas and analyses through newsletters, letters to stakeholders, and informational notices through various media outlets, newspaper columns, and agency reports. Like all scientists, sociologists of sport and physical activity who work in an academic research setting have a responsibility to share their new knowledge with the general population, not only with other academic professionals. Increasingly, academic professionals attempt a threefold approach to communicating about their research and prepare a publication or presentation for three audiences: academic peers, allied practitioners, and community members.

Techniques for Sociological Knowledge Construction

Building on the three categories of knowledge production described previously—landscape, experience, and analytic—let us now turn to more specific information on methods or techniques for creating new knowledge in the sociology of sport and physical activity. There is considerable overlap between these components, and most social scientists move back and forth across categories in order to produce meaningful, timely, and relevant knowledge.

Landscape Knowledge Techniques

Specific techniques commonly used to produce landscape knowledge include surveys of large sample populations, community case studies, and regular census surveys (e.g., U.S. Census every 10 years). Surveys generally include focused questions around a particular topic, like the one conducted annually by the Sporting Goods Manufacturers Association that asks about physical activity involvement, equipment purchased, and expert services used in the past year. You have likely encountered many informal or unscientific surveys in social media applications and on the Internet. These are more like casual polls; they are not the same as scientific techniques for survey. Still, social scientists do conduct scientific surveys in multiple formats, such as paper and pencil, telephone, or online. It is not the medium that determines rigor; it is the application of the scientific method throughout the entire research endeavor. This latter point is true for all of the methods described here.

Within the landscape mode of knowledge production, a community case study may also employ survey techniques but will likely do so in concert with other techniques, such as document analysis (e.g., public policy or health information brochures), community mapping of research-related sites and resources, and perhaps secondary data such as health statistics by the Centers for Disease Control and Prevention or other big databases that offer community-based information.

In terms of U.S. healthful living, the Framingham Heart Study (from Framingham, Massachusetts) has long been a community case study of health behaviors and longitudinal health outcomes. **Longitudinal** means conducted over an extended period, such as a lifetime or perhaps over generations. The health data from this Northeastern community are a key information resource for the general population.

STUDYING FANTASY SPORT PARTICIPANTS

Ruihley and Billings (2012) surveyed 530 fantasy sport participants about their media consumption and motivations for participation. They were especially interested in how male and female fans differed in their sport fandom, media consumption, and fantasy sport motivations. They created a Fantasy Sport Questionnaire Scale that included items related to arousal, enjoyment, entertainment, escape, pastimes, self-esteem, surveillance, fandom, Mavenism, and Schwabism.

Men ($N = 348$) reported consuming 21.3 hours of sport content per week, while women ($N = 182$) consumed only 11.6 hours. Men had higher levels of sport fandom as determined by the number of years involved in fantasy sport, the number of leagues they participate in, and hours devoted to their fantasy sport participation. The results were in agreement for men and women related to motivations for participation, with men listing enjoyment, entertainment, and surveillance as their top three reasons. Women listed the same three, although in a different order, with entertainment first, then surveillance and enjoyment. While the men in the study found sport to be their primary outlet for entertainment and enjoyment, women identified sport as one of many outlets for their entertainment.

1. Do you know anyone who participates in fantasy sport?

2. How do the findings help you to explain their (or your own) participation?

In a much more generalized manner, the U.S. Bureau of the Census conducts one of the largest surveys in the world every 10 years. Although the Bureau attempts to survey a majority of U.S. households and use a rigorous scientific method, the resulting data are not comprehensive. These data are generalizable, or determined to adequately reflect the characteristics of the broad population. Data sets of this size aid policy makers and program planners in thinking about resources for physical activity, such as indoor and outdoor space, types of equipment, and likely rates of use. These sorts of survey items often allow only responses from among set choices, not write-in, original responses.

longitudinal—A study that has been conducted over an extended period, such as a lifetime or perhaps over generations.

Experience Knowledge Techniques

Experience approaches to knowledge production may also use the techniques mentioned previously, but they do so with a distinguishing goal in mind—to learn about the actual experiences of people in sport and physical activity settings. Although a survey may be used in experience mode of knowledge production, it goes far beyond counting things. Instead, surveys focus on the ways informants might describe their own interactions, access points, and social support systems related to their physical activity.

For example, rather than simply asking informants how often they participate in a physical activity, a social scientist seeking to understand the experience of sport and physical activity might ask them to describe a key aspect of a particular event or to recall and describe a feeling related to a physical activity experience. Given this focus on participant-centered understandings of experience, social scientists may use interview techniques in addition to the survey and case study techniques already described. Interviews can take on various formats, such as individual, dyads (2 people), or small groups (typically 4 to 8 people).

The style of interaction between researcher and research participant can vary as well, with some being guided by a standard set of focused questions and others inviting a storytelling sort of response (offering minimal guidance as the informant tells their story). Imagine how this type of open narrative interview might produce very different stories even from the same event. For example, a social scientist may wish to understand the experience of youth soccer league involvement and may conduct interviews with the participant, one friend who is not on the team, the parents, and the league director. The social scientist could pose a common set of questions to each informant or could simply proceed by asking informants to "tell the story

Quick Fact

In 2009, FX debuted the sitcom comedy *The League*, which chronicles the daily lives of members of a fantasy football league. The league is mostly made up of men but includes one of their wives. The television show revealed how sport, even fantasy sport, can be a misogynistic space. The television series ran for seven seasons, ending in 2015.

of youth soccer in this community today." As you imagine the different kinds of knowledge that will be gained regarding experience of sport and physical activity, also consider how such data may reflect a sociological imagination.

Analytic Knowledge Techniques

When the research goal is one of deep theoretical analyses, the techniques for knowledge production shift a bit to focus on symbolic meaning and cultural significance of sport and physical activity. In the previous two categories, social scientists' goal is to identify something real or material, like the rates of participation (landscape) or the actual experience of sport and physical activity (experience). In analytic mode of knowledge production, the focus is on cultural meanings and values related to sport and physical activity. Thus, rather than studying the actual experiences in that youth soccer league, a social scientist working in analytic mode will study the cultural significance of youth soccer in an entire community, in several communities, or in a national or global context.

This type of research may also use those techniques previously described, but it typically also requires integration of techniques, time in the field of inquiry, and depth of broad, sociocultural context. A social scientist may conduct an ethnographic study of a town and its value for sport or physical activity, such as of *Friday Night Lights* (Bissinger, 1990), which was an ethnography of Texas high school football before it became a popular book, film, and television show. H.G. Bissinger spent two years in Odessa, Texas, studying high school football. He described its value and place in this community, both on and off the field. He also described football in the context of economic conditions, educational policy, race and gender relations, local newspaper framings, and various social statuses within the town. This is an example of analytic knowledge production.

Recall that the broad field of exercise and sport science has long been cross-disciplinary in nature, yet it has relied largely on **positivism**, or a highly rational way of posing and studying questions that features a belief in scientific objectivity and linear progression as bases for its primary inquiry framework. As subdisciplinary areas, especially those connected to the social sciences, have advanced, so too have new paradigmatic approaches to the study of human movement, physical activity, and the body. There remains little meaning in attempts to know about the body without accounting for context, space, time, and place. Although landscape and experience types of knowledge remain useful in the sociological study of human physical activity, they are only two choices in a range of inquiry traditions and study designs that produce various types of knowledge.

Research in the sociology of sport and physical activity requires and provokes consideration of the variety of analytic strategies and inquiry tools from which researchers may choose. In this sense, social science approaches often draw our attention *away* from mechanistic, technical aspects of inquiry (data collection) and begin with a focus on worldviews or overarching frameworks that shape the entire process of identifying meaningful questions. David Andrews (2008) argues that the study of the body cannot be

positivism—An approach to knowledge production that favors objectivity, observable linear progress, and precise, predetermined operational definitions.

reduced to the biological framing of bodily performance. Rather, he reminds us that "the active body is as much a social, cultural, philosophical, and historical entity as it is a genetic, physiological, and psychological vessel and needs to be engaged as such through rigorous ethnographic, autoethnographic, textual and discursive, socio-historic treatment" (p. 49).

Through the application of various theoretical perspectives, the use of a variety of data-generation techniques, and an intentional practice of communicating findings with at least three levels of audience, sociologists of sport and physical activity are able to study and explain the paradoxes of sport and much, much more. Clearly, producing meaningful, socially useful knowledge is hard work! Regardless of the overarching framework or specific methods used, it is incredibly demanding to identify a meaningful question, deploy the best set of research tools, and explain one's findings in an ethically informative and accessible manner. This may sound daunting, but it is also very interesting and some of the most fun a person can have!

The sociology of sport and physical activity presents unique challenges and opportunities for those willing to develop the proper skills for conducting research. The remainder of this book describes academically legitimized forms of knowledge production and everyday ways to assess the role of sport and physical activity in one's community. Both formal research and everyday interaction with research

 HOW SOCIOLOGISTS OF SPORT AND PHYSICAL ACTIVITY COLLECT DATA

Surveys can be useful in determining how people feel and think about a topic, such as cheating, athletes as role models, and the issue of performance-enhancing drugs (PEDs), but also in determining how often someone exercises or watches sports on television, as well as the amount of money they spend on sport or physical activity items.

1. Develop a mini-survey with at least five questions about a sport- or exercise-related topic. You can have questions with yes/no responses or a range extending from strongly agree to strongly disagree. Ask 20 classmates to complete your survey. What conclusions can you draw from your responses? How might you change your questions for a future survey?

2. Observe a movement setting for 60 minutes. Take field notes throughout the hour. For this activity, do not take notes at something that you are also a participant in. Participation makes it very challenging to take notes and observe. This should not be done from memory. That is, these notes should be something you observe now, not something you watched last semester or a year ago or even a week ago. Your field notes should have details—what did you see, hear, overhear, or wonder? Consider what you knew prior to heading into the hour about the setting and people in the setting. What themes or concepts do you see emerging in your setting?

findings are crucial to a sociological understanding of the meaning and value of sport and physical activity. Social scientists use a range of methods within a range of methodological and theoretical frameworks.

Thinking Beyond Sport

If you recall from chapter 1, the evolution of the field included an early focus on sport, but more recent interest in other sporting spaces includes physical education, leisure, exercise programs, and health-related physical activity. The reasons for including these spaces include the fact that not all members of society participate in what we call sport. Many people participate in various forms of physical activity; types of human interaction change with different forms of physical activity; and different goals, values, and governing structures shape human experiences in each of these forms of physical activity. Thus, the remainder of this book considers three contextual spaces: sporting spaces, schooling spaces, and exercising spaces. This perspective makes it possible to study the fluid, constantly changing contexts for human physical activity in varied social spaces. Surely, from your own experience, it is abundantly clear that human physical activity looks different in a sport league than in a PE class or a fitness center. It is our goal to help you discover the commonalities and differences in these spaces.

 PARADOXES OF SPORT

Sociologist D. Stanley Eitzen created the following list of paradoxes in sport (2002). Eitzen's list illustrates the strange ways sport can seem to be contradictory, providing a variety of experiences for its participants.

What examples can you come up with that illustrate Eitzen's list of paradoxes?

Paradox 1: Sport is both unifying and divisive.

Paradox 2: Sport is inclusive and exclusive.

Paradox 3: Sport is fair and sport is foul.

Paradox 4: Sport is healthy; sport is destructive.

Paradox 5: Sport is expressive; sport is controlling.

Paradox 6: Sport is equity; sport is difference.

Paradox 7: Sport is educational; sport is a money-making, masculinizing distraction.

Paradox 8: Sport is a path to upward social mobility; sport is a holding place for otherwise marginalized members of society.

Paradox 9: Sport is an economic engine for cities; sport is an economic drain on taxpayers.

Quick Fact

Girls on the Run is a national program for girls aged 8 to 13. Teams of girls train with coaches to prepare for a 5K at the conclusion of the season. Running is used as a physical activity to motivate girls to enjoy physical activity, and the program serves as a space for girls to receive healthy and positive messages about their bodies. Trained coaches lead girls through a 24-lesson curriculum and running program. There are more than 200 Girls on the Run programs across the United States. For more on this organization, see www.girlsontherun.org.

The Short of It

- Sociological skills and knowledge around sport and physical activity may inform your work as a physical educator, leisure professional, athletic trainer, or coach, as well as your own political activism as a citizen who values meaningful physical activity for all members of society.

- Sociologists of sport and physical activity unveil the ways that sport reflects a range of conditions that exist in society, not to undermine sport or physical activity but to enable us to enhance this crucial, provocative, and exciting aspect of social life and human interaction.

- The range of application of sociological knowledge around sport and physical activity is somewhat artificially split by advocacy, allied professional practice, and academic professional practice. Each of these is a crucial application of sociological knowledge.

- A person with interest and knowledge in both how human beings move and what this movement means in different moments and under changing social conditions can bridge divides between natural and social sciences and can help promote a society where meaningful physical activity is accessible to all.

- The most prominent scientific tools for social scientists are theories (structural, cultural, and interactionist) about the way society functions, analytic strategies for sociological analyses (landscape, experience, and analytic), and communication of findings (professional journals, books, and community newsletters).

- Sociologists of sport and physical activity today aim their analyses at three contextual spaces: sporting spaces, schooling spaces, and exercising spaces.

II

PART

Building Blocks of Sociology of Sport and Physical Activity

Part II engages you in key issues in particular sporting, schooling, and exercising spaces. It discusses research findings and key questions in the field as they relate to each of three common social spaces for physical activity. This part describes the range and depth of sociological analyses in sport and physical activity. Chapter 3 describes the ways that sport and physical activity constantly interact with major spheres of social life, such as religion, education, political structures, medicine, mass media, and the economy. Related to the power of these major spheres of life, chapter 4 focuses on the ways that bodies and embodiment are governed and experienced in sociocultural contexts. Chapters 5 and 6 describe and discuss diversity and difference in local, global, national, and international settings. Chapter 7 presents the role of sport and physical activity in social change. Part II concludes with an epilogue that presents ideas about the future of sociological knowledge in sport and physical activity, including how the field may best respond to changing societal conditions.

CHAPTER 3

Sport, Physical Activity, and the Major Spheres of Life

In this chapter you will learn the following:

✓ How sociologists make sense of culture and structure
✓ How societies attempt to create stability in everyday life
✓ How major spheres of life shape our daily interactions
✓ The interaction of sport and physical activity with major spheres of life

> I don't think of the laws as rules you have to follow, but more as suggestions.
>
> **Comedian George Carlin**

Imagine you are at your younger sibling's tee ball game. It is obvious to you that even though this is an organized sport league, it is also a place where families gather and where goods and services are exchanged, dominant ideas and values are reinforced, school communities are extended, and certain religious practices are respected (e.g., games on Saturday rather than Sunday). Each of these influences in this sporting space constitutes a major sphere of social life. Sociologists of sport and physical activity regularly study these spheres, including sport, as social systems that reflect both structural and cultural elements of the social world. To extend your emergent sociological imagination, we now invite you to consider how societies operate, including what constitutes their major working parts, how these parts work together, and how sport and physical activity work in concert with these major societal components.

For sociologists, **major spheres of life** are those formal ways of organizing social life that shape our everyday interactions (sometimes referred to as major social institutions). These major spheres of life are crucial building blocks to a sociological imagination of sport and physical activity. Specifically, sociologists of sport and physical activity seek to explain how these major spheres influence our daily lives as well as the interdependent nature of their relationship with sport and physical activity. A quick recall of any personal experience in sport, leisure, exercise, or physical education will surely include interactions with people, agencies, policies, and social groups, just to name a few. The more you apply your sociological lens, the more these external influences become obvious as part of your lifelong physical activity choices and experiences.

Still, one might ask what the major spheres of social life are or why we have major spheres of life. Well, to be sure, all societies face problems. Thus, all societies seek solutions. Major spheres of life emerge and change in response to these needs in order to offer a certain amount of structure to everyday life. As one example, the **economy** is a major sphere of social life. In the United States, most adults work roughly 34 hours per week, five days per week (Organisation for Economic Co-operation and Development, 2016). There is nothing natural about this, but it is considered "normal." We are all expected to work full time for much of our adult life until we retire in order to earn money that we then spend on things like food, housing, health care, transportation, and entertainment. Therefore, our relation to the economy and labor force has a significant influence on how we structure non-work time, interact with family and friends, meet personal needs and non-work obligations, and engage in physical activity and even how we view ourselves in society as a whole.

For sociologists of sport and physical activity, this is also true. Much of the sport studies scholarship illuminates the structures (working parts and hierarchies) of sport and physical activity spaces. One way to do this is to examine the interconnectedness of major spheres of life and sport. We describe several examples in this chapter, but first let's take a look at how these spheres of life accomplish their goals of stabilizing our daily lives.

When social scientists talk about major spheres of life, they are referring to a desire for all societies to create and maintain stability in everyday ways of life. As one example, family—not yours or mine, but the social institution of **family**—has developed differently in different places around the world as a standard way of meeting a particular set of basic needs, often featuring regulation of sexual relations and maintenance of a population. Family structures profoundly influence individual lives in structural and cultural ways, and their influence is often beyond our ordinary awareness. For example, in the United States, families are quite diverse in structure, but in large part, they typically represent a household in which one or more adults contribute to the household income and two or more children are cared for (e.g., fed, clothed, and sent to school). Laws and policies exist that constitute who counts as family and how the social welfare program will support families. Families are resources for neighborhoods, school and work communities, and political structures. On the cultural side of the sociological equation, community events are often described as "family friendly," and employers and businesses often suggest that their workers are like family. There is a dominant cultural sense that family members care for and support each other and offer a haven from an otherwise cruel, demanding world (Collier, Rosaldo, & Yanagisako, 1992; Thorne, 1992). In reality, families are also demanding, requiring various types of labor from members and holding out rewards and penalties for one's performance of their family roles. It is the influence of this institution or social system—family—that makes it a major sphere of life and places it in interaction with other major spheres to shape our daily social interactions, at times aiding us with stability and other times challenging us with limitations.

Major spheres of social life are more specifically described as an organized interrelated set of normative elements that guide behavior of members of society, helping them to define and follow norms, values, and role expectations. Members of society devise major spheres of social life and pass these on to succeeding generations to provide

major spheres of life—Social science reference to the components of social systems that exert an external influence on individual lives. Major spheres of life in U.S. society include families, religion, education, politics, economy, and media.

economy—A process of producing and consuming wealth and resources in a social system.

family—A basic social unit often consisting of two adult parents and their children.

 Quick Fact

On average, Americans spend 90,000 hours at work throughout their lifetimes. Roughly 25 percent of people check in with work while on vacation, using e-mail or a cell phone (Shontel, 2011).

functionalist perspective—A social science theory suggesting that all components of society serve a function and that all components can work harmoniously to serve members of society.

conflict theory—A social science theory that claims that societies exist in an ongoing state of conflict due to competition for a limited set of resources.

socialization—A process of learning the customs, values, and attitudes of a social group.

permanent solutions for crucial societal problems (Eitzen & Sage, 2008). In the United States, youth are expected to attend school, which not only provides members of society with an education but also reflects a patterned arrangement that regulates the kinds of knowledge gained and the purpose for gaining it. As a result, education as a major sphere of life is about much more than content knowledge—it is also about learning how to be a proper citizen both in and beyond the school setting. A quick pondering of the other lessons learned in school might reveal how to obey authority, follow rules, collaborate, and work independently. Even in physical education and school-based sports, it is likely you have observed the lesson beyond the physical skill, such as following directions or acting in ways that benefit the group, not only one's self. Many scholars suggest that kids in U.S. schools are often imagined as in-process adults—they are not simply children but are learning how to become adult citizens (Burrows & Wright, 2004).

Seeing Social Life as Harmonious or Conflictual

A **functionalist perspective** is a macro view, or a lens on the whole society and its major working parts. This perspective begins with an assertion that the major parts of a society work in harmony to meet the needs of all citizens. Sociologists who follow a functionalist perspective argue that major spheres of life contribute to the maintenance and functioning of the entire social system in five specific ways:

- Replace members (family)
- Teach new members (education)
- Produce and distribute goods and services (economy)
- Preserve order (politics/nation-state)
- Provide a sense of purpose (religion)

In an opposing view of how society works, **conflict theorists** argue that in all societies, there are shifts in economic systems that create unequal opportunity structures. Therefore, classes of society are always competing for limited resources—typically, those with access to capital resources (which could mean money or other financial assets) and those without access. Due to this conflict, the five spheres of social life previously listed represent a social system that works better for some citizens and not so well for others. The focus here is not on theoretical differences but rather on the important role of sport in major spheres of life, an aspect of social

I never joined the Boy Scouts. I don't trust any organization that has a handbook.

Comedian George Carlin

systems on which both functionalists and conflict theorists can agree. Regardless of one's theoretical leanings, identifying and explaining the core components of social systems are fundamental to all knowledge projects in sociology.

The passing along of all of these lessons—in schools, families, and church settings and through policies, mass-mediated images, and ideas—is known as **socialization**. For sociologists, socialization is not hanging out with friends and having a

 # YOUTH SPORT

Most of America's youth sport programs have origins in the public school system. The first organized sport leagues for boys were established at the beginning of the 20th century. Those boys would hardly recognize youth sport today! Youth sport, once located within public schools and sponsored by city parks and recreation departments, is thriving in a club sport system where parents pay thousands of dollars for their child's membership on a youth sport team. The youth sport industry is now valued at just over $5 billion. The Little League World Series is televised on ESPN, and high school football and basketball games and their athletes are routinely written about in national sporting magazines. Whereas character building and fun were once the principles guiding youth sport, most parents, athletes, and coaches are now focused on winning. Expectations are greater due to the time and money invested in youth sport.

1. How has youth sport changed since your participation?

2. How might youth sport experiences vary depending on sport? Geographic region? Socioeconomic status? Gender? Two-parent versus single-parent households?

Youth sports have become increasingly focused on athleticism instead of character building and fun.

capitalist society—A society that is organized around an economic structure based on a belief in a beneficial relationship between producing goods and buying and using goods. Capitalism has changed over time, and the core relationship between production of goods and use of goods continues to raise new questions for social scientists.

good time—that is *socializing*. The sociological concept of socialization refers to a complicated process of transmitting societal norms, values, and beliefs to society's members. This transmission is accomplished through the structure of major spheres of social life and individual human interactions within those spheres.

Our socialization is never complete. In fact, throughout our lives, we are in a constant process of socializing into, through, and out of particular social contexts. Moreover, dominant societal values influence the structure of all major spheres of social life and vice versa, and they are based on our political and economic system. In the United States, a **capitalist society**, all major spheres of social life both reflect and are influenced by a set of capitalist-inspired values.

These are the typically referenced capitalist-inspired values:

- Success: winning out over all others
- Competition: learning to be the best, not just good
- Means of achievement: hard work, continual striving, deferred gratification
- Progress: examples are technology, constant improvement
- Materialism: value based on accumulation of things, money, lifestyle
- External conformity: willingness to go along ("work the system and the system works")

Learning to See the Interdependence of Sport and Major Spheres of Life

Sport is interdependent on the major spheres of life, which are family, economy, politics, education, mass media, and religion. In this section, we explain the relationships between sport and each sphere. Many of our examples will be familiar to you, and you may begin to notice your own ability to identify the various ways sport interacts with these other major institutions of society.

Sport, Physical Activity, and Family

Sociologists have spent a lot of time studying families and the role of sport and physical activity in families. Early research indicated that parents were the main influence in decisions about sport involvement. Referring to parents as socializing agents, scientists further detailed how gender and age influenced this role of parents, and the possibility that parents may also be socialized into sport through their children. Studying sport in family settings added complexity and clarity to sociological knowledge in family systems in general. For example, Susan Greendorfer (1983) studied the role of mothers and fathers in socializing their male and female children into sport.

Beyond the sport involvement question, sociologists have examined family and sport in terms of economic conditions, labor required to maintain sport involvement, and family systems as conducive or restrictive in terms of physical activity involvement. A most interesting book by Shona Thompson (1999) called *Mother's Taxi* details the labor of adult women in heterosexual couples where all family members participated in the sport of tennis. In her ethnographic analyses, Thompson was able to demonstrate the amount of hidden labor in family sport involvement. In this case, the majority of the labor was done by the mom in the family. Even when the moms played tennis, they had fund-raisers, youth programs, and social gatherings at the tennis club that required their labor beyond the tennis court. Fathers and children were largely removed from this and typical household labor, including laundry, meal preparation, equipment maintenance, and scheduling of family involvement in tennis. These two examples of the role of sport in the family sphere ought to raise new ideas about the interdependence of sport and family.

Sociology of sport and physical activity also indicates an interdependence of sport and family. This simply suggests the many ways that sport depends on family systems and that family systems depend on sport. These major spheres of life interact in daily activities to ensure that the stability work of the family system is accomplished. Families depend on youth sport leagues to extend the school day and offer adult supervision throughout the day. Some families depend on corporate or professional sport for entertainment and time for interacting with family members.

Sport, Physical Activity, and the Economy

As many sociologists of sport have pointed out, all levels of sport are increasingly commodified or in some way tied to making a financial profit (Zirin, 2013). Those who apply a sociological lens to their study of sport and physical activity examine the ways sport relies on and responds to changing economic conditions as well as

OCCUPATIONAL HAZARDS FOR PROFESSIONAL FOOTBALL (SOCCER) PLAYERS

Roderick (2012) conducted interviews with 49 professional football (soccer) players to examine the issues related to job relocation and how decision making is conducted in families. It is common for a professional athlete to play for several teams over a career, so most athletes are likely to experience the issue of job relocation. Roderick's interest was in the relationship between the work space and family life. Many athletes and their partners acknowledged that living apart is an occupational hazard, and some viewed commuting as another solution. Whereas wives were more likely to follow their partners in the past, many contemporary relationships were more egalitarian, which resulted in the athlete commuting between work and home to provide a more stable environment for the family and to maintain social networks. Often times, we don't give much thought to the workings and family dynamics of athletes—or coaches.

What sort of questions could we ask that would help us better understand the challenges faced by the families of athletes and coaches?

> ## Quick Fact
> Families with children who participate in sports report higher levels of family satisfaction (Sabo & Veliz, 2008).

the ways the global economy relies on sport as a site for production and consumption, or making products, marketing those products, and providing a space in which people will buy and use those products. Economists and political scientists have, at times, turned their attention to sport and the economy, offering analyses of job creation and economic effects of sport arenas in major U.S. cities (Noll & Zimbalist, 1997) as well as more global analyses of the working conditions in Nike shoe manufacturing plants (Enloe, 2004; Sage, 2010).

Economic relations have always been complicated, and in the current day of fast-paced, electronic, global transfers of money, goods, and services, they are newly complex. This new complexity is both exciting and concerning for sociologists of sport and physical activity. For example, the emergence of transnational corporations that employ millions of people around the world has created a game of tug-of-war between governments and corporate entities.

The interdependence of sport and the global economy is illuminated through the study of trade agreements, sporting goods manufacturing, regional and global taxes on profits, and employment requirements, to name a few key components (Jackson, Batty, & Scherer, 2001; Sage, 2010).

Political scientist Cynthia Enloe put sport directly into a critical political and feminist understanding of globalization and its consequences. She identified several sneaker manufacturers, not only Nike, in her discussion of the ways that constantly changing international trade agreements (and connections to regulating agencies like the IMF and World Bank) create political spaces where a person's labor becomes "cheapened" for the profit of multinational corporations (2004, p. 60). In a veiled manner, women (especially young versus older, unmarried versus married, and rural versus urban women) are pitted against each other in a world economy that continues to treat women's labor as extra or necessary only when male workers are not available. The subcontracting of factory work removes legal responsibility from **multinational corporations** (like Nike) and reinvents a narrative of corrupt, underdeveloped postcolonial nations who need jobs from more developed nations so much that they are willing to mistreat their own people. On the other end of this economic, political, and cultural exchange are the upwardly mobile middle-class Americans and Europeans who travel the globe in pursuit of meaningful sporting experiences . . . wearing those Nike sneakers during their Great Wall of China marathon, at their Caribbean resort health club, or at their mountaineering base camp in Nepal.

This economic tug-of-war is relevant in sport and physical activity as well. Some governments require regular physical activity for school-age citizens and some for adults as well.

multinational corporation—A corporation that has facilities and other resources in one or more countries other than their home-office country.

state—The social system structure of governance—not just elected officials but all the structures of law and order that govern our daily social interactions.

⏳ ATHLETE SALARIES

In 1981, New Orleans Saints quarterback Archie Manning earned $600,000, the equivalent to $1.53 million in 2013. In 1970, the average salary in MLB was $20,000, jumping to $2.6 million in 2005, with a league minimum of $316,000. Twenty years ago, the average NBA salary was $575,000, and has increased to $5.2 million. Tiger Woods is the first athlete to earn more than $1 billion as a result of tournament winnings and endorsements. Most individual sport athletes, including those in action sports, earn prize money for winning tournaments and contests, but they also enhance their earnings through endorsements. Team sport athletes have greater salaries, based less on winning and more on contracts, though some have performance clauses that reward individual achievements. The average American's compensation has not increased at the same rate as that of professional athletes (or CEOs, for that matter, another group that has enjoyed a tremendous increase in compensation over the last 30 years). How much money are team owners making to be able to pay their employees (players) this much money?

Other nations do not fund and regulate daily physical activity for their citizens; instead, it is a private, self-funded matter. Applying a sociological imagination to this means asking what kinds of social interactions and structures of sport and physical activity are able to develop under these different economic conditions.

Sport, Physical Activity, and Politics

In sport studies, the most common focus around sport and politics has been on sport and nationalism, or the ways that sport becomes representative of the nation. Most often, social scientists put their focus on the government and on state-sponsored policies that influence how citizens engage in sport and physical activity. For example, the UK has a national physical education curriculum and socialist health care policy, while the United States has no national curriculum for physical education and only recently has attempted to create a health care policy that is accessible to all citizens. These may seem like random policies that have very little to do with your own choices for daily physical activity, but to the extent that these policies are directly tied to funding of local agencies, decisions about what gets taught in public schools, and people's perceived ability to maintain their health, they greatly influence the physical activity of all citizens.

For sociologists, the term **state** refers to structures of governance in society and applies a sort of order to daily life that goes beyond any order that could be applied by individual citizens. This concept does not refer solely to government, nor does it refer to any specific state within a nation; rather, it refers to national and supranational structures that govern behavior and interaction of citizens. In this sense, the state has the authority to generate and apply collective power, especially toward its aims to ensure law, order, stability, conflict resolution, common defense, and public welfare for its citizens. The state is said to be interdependent with sport. Among the examples of this interdependence are the professional sport exemptions from antitrust laws, which treat professional sports differently than other corporate entities and place the state in a policy position of protecting the right of certain sport businesses to hold a monopoly in that business (e.g., MLB). Other examples of state support of sport include public subsidizing of stadiums, which means taxpayer dollars contribute to building the venues where corporate sport team owners and league officials host games and make a profit. As well, when a city is selected to host the Olympic Games or even more regional events like elite youth soccer tournaments, the local host is expected to make their public facilities and public safety resources available to the event. These investments in sporting events are everyday examples of the ways that sport benefits from its interdependence with the state.

While the state invests in these sporting spaces and events, it also benefits from such arrangements. For example, in this relationship, the state relies on sporting events to promote national identity and build community. Consider the use of Yankee

 ## ARTHUR ASHE, ATHLETE AND ACTIVIST

© Associated Press

Arthur Ashe is remembered as a champion tennis player, but he contributed to sport beyond simply being a good athlete. Ashe was born and raised in segregated Richmond, Virginia, where his access to public tennis courts was limited. In 1963, Ashe was the first African American player to be selected to the Davis Cup team, representing the United States in tournament play. He was awarded a scholarship to play tennis at the University of California at Los Angeles, where he won the NCAA title in 1965, the same year his team won the team title. He became the first African American male to win the U.S. Open title in 1968 and went on to win two other Grand Slam titles in his career. Ashe was denied a visa to play tennis in South Africa in 1969. As a result, he became heavily involved in fighting the apartheid movement of South Africa, using sport as one tool to work against the racist policies of the government.

In 1993, Ashe authored a three-volume set about African American sport history, *A Hard Road to Glory: A History of the African American Athlete,* as well as his coauthored memoir with Arnold Rampersad, *Days of Glory,* which detailed his struggles with racism throughout his life and his health problems related to acquiring AIDS, which led to his premature death in early 1993. While he rose to fame as a tennis player, Ashe is remembered for his political activism and for serving as a public face for AIDS in its early days, when many people associated the disease with homosexual men and IV drug users (he acquired it through a blood transfusion during a surgery). He is a member of several halls of fame, has been memorialized on a U.S. postage stamp and with a statue in Richmond, appearing on the same avenue with Confederate heroes.

I felt like, if anything, we gave people a break from what was going on. . . . It was, "Hey, we can watch the Giants." I felt pressure to win in Kansas City . . . but more important was playing in a way that would make people proud. That we won the game was an added bonus. It was nice to know that . . . we had a positive influence on the events that were going on.

Kerry Collins, 2001 New York Giants quarterback,
after the World Trade Center attack on September 11, 2001

Stadium for a multidenominational event marking unity and healing following the events of September 11, 2001, or the use of the Houston Astrodome as a temporary shelter after the devastating blow of Hurricane Katrina—two vivid moments where sporting spaces became community spaces in very different ways. Of course, we may also consider the Los Angeles Summer Games in 1984 as a moment when hosting the Olympic Games became tied to corporate investment and profit. Consider more local examples in your own community. Are there sporting events to commemorate a person or moment of interest to your local community? Applying our sociological imagination, we must also consider the powerful ways that the state relies on sport. Throughout history, the state has depended on major sporting events, especially international events, to deliver propaganda or messages about the superiority of the nation. The state has also used sporting events to distract the masses from a focus on other societal issues. Celebrating Title IX may distract us from recognizing that in the United States, women still earn $.78 for every $1 earned by a male worker (Hegewisch, Williams, Hartmann, & Hudiberg, 2014). In this example, the state benefits from our preference to celebrate women's advancement in sport rather than rally for pay equity. Finally, the state also benefits from its interdependence with sport by having a space to ease members of society into difficult social change, like race relations in the United States or the dismantling of apartheid in South Africa. In both of these examples, sport became a social space where people could take steps toward these changes. Intentional or not, the state benefitted from these sporting spaces and was perhaps better able to usher in societal-level policy change.

The nation also aligns with supranational structures, like the International Olympic Committee (IOC), to serve interdependent needs. Nations rely on the Olympic Games as a space for demonstrating their greatness both on the athletic

 Quick Fact

The gender wage gap is also a race and gender wage gap: Latinas earn 54 cents of every dollar earned by a White male. African American women earn 64 cents, Native Hawaiian and Pacific Islander women earn 65 cents, American Indian and Alaska Native women earn 59 cents, and Asian American women earn 90 cents of that same White male dollar (Fisher, 2015).

TAKING SPORT SERIOUSLY

How do we know that sport is an important and powerful cultural institution in American culture? This brainstorming activity asks you to identify the evidence one might present to support the claim that sport is, in fact, a major institution in American society, similar to the major spheres of life. If sport were put on trial for being a powerful influence on American ideas, society, and culture, what evidence would you present to the jury to help support this argument?

List 15 pieces of evidence that sport is a major institution in American culture.

field and beyond. Achievement on the global athletic field is believed to indicate a great nation, one that produces citizens who are capable of great things. The Olympic Games provide a world stage for nations to demonstrate their skill in world sports and in some cases their uniqueness through talents in regional sports. Consider who dominates the Summer Games versus the Winter Games. The IOC relies on nations to provide the drama of the Games and to represent themselves as unique yet willing members of a world community. The opening and closing ceremonies depend on these national differences and global commonality to remind viewers of the importance of the Games to world harmony. In table 3.1, we suggest some of the benefits received by the International Olympic Committee as related to the six spheres of life in society. What are examples of additional benefits for the IOC?

TABLE 3.1   Interdependence of the IOC and Major Spheres of Life (MSL)

Major spheres of life	IOC benefits	MSL in action
Family	Support of athletes/workers	Provides stability for members and produces new members
Economy	Sponsors, concessions, broadcasting fees, volunteer labor	Creates spaces for paid labor and consumption
Politics	Nations want to host Games	Promotes a nationalist agenda
Education	Introduction to sport skills, early training of future elite athletes	Prepares members of society
Mass media	Advertising, marketing, mass communication	Dissemination of information, sharing of ideas
Religion	Adds transcendence to Games	Ritualistic recognition of significant human life events, such as marriage, birth, and death

Sport, Physical Activity, and Education

The United States, more than many other nations, ties sport to educational institutions. Education, as a major sphere of social life, is a crucial space in which citizens learn content and ways of interacting—lessons that aid people in becoming full citizens in their communities and in the social world. As a social system, education has changed over time to meet changing needs in critical historic moments, like industrialization, or the major shift from small agricultural communal living to large urban-centered living. During the industrial revolution, the U.S. education system shifted from using one-room school houses like those featured in *Little House on the Prairie* to school districts of varying sizes and resources. As formal education developed in the United States, so too did the need to add health and physical education to the daily curriculum. Historians, sociologists, and anthropologists who study physical culture have chronicled the role of sport and physical activity in the evolution of education and have studied things such as changing focus on physical education lessons throughout history; social statuses in PE classrooms related to social categories of gender, race, religion, and ability; and the role of the body in public spheres. Doug Foley's (1999) research on high school football and the rituals that go along with it illuminated the role of sport in producing school culture for both sport participants and nonparticipants. In some ways, football is implicated in exacerbating inequalities (e.g., a hierarchy of athletes and nonathletes); in other ways, the sport team creates at least the illusion of community in challenging space (e.g., school pride and school-wide rituals like pep rallies). Recall the work of H.G. Bissinger mentioned in chapter 2 that offered similar analyses of the role of football in school and town communities.

Sport and education are clearly interdependent, especially in the U.S. educational system. Education relies on sport and physical activity for creating community and enhancing behavior and academic performance. If we return to the Olympic Games as our common example, we can see the presence of Olympic heroes and their performances used in schools to promote the aforementioned goals—the IOC

 HIGH SCHOOL SPORTS AND TAX DOLLARS

Ripley (2013) explained that the United States spends more tax monies on high school athletics than on math and science. And we wonder why our high school students lag behind their international peers. Her article makes the case against high school sports, and her argument is compelling (especially when we consider that Americans are generally very opposed to socialism, yet the tax support for high school sports is a perfect example of socialism in practice).

1. What would happen if communities and school boards decided to no longer financially support high school athletics?

2. How would teams continue to participate?

3. Which sports would survive the cuts?

even provides information and educational materials on their website. In turn, the IOC relies on educational systems to introduce young people to a variety of sports and to provide increasingly elite performance spaces. Many Olympic athletes enter sports initially through physical education or after-school sports teams. The USOC hosts Olympic Development Leagues that extend high school leagues in particular sports and offer a more elite space for skill development. These leagues typically hold their practices and contests on school property, which is another example of interdependence of public educational resources and corporate sport structures.

Sport, Physical Activity, and the Mass Media

When social scientists study the mass media as a major sphere of social life, they are referring to "all technically organized means of communication that reach large numbers of people quickly and effectively" (Sage, 1998, p. 159). Some scholars focus on the mass media's role as a public service that meets the communication needs of a global social world, while others turn their analytic attention to the mass media as deeply engaged with corporate and state agendas in the production of preferred information and news. Others consider the manner in which the mass media exercises a certain power in society, especially as this power demonstrates its interconnections with other major spheres of social life.

The mass media exercises communicative and cultural power through four specific privileges (Coakley, 2009). First, recognized media outlets enjoy constitutional protection as they seek access to news and unfolding events and stories. Freedom of the press is deeply valued in American society, which we imagine to be open, and so we attempt to maintain spaces for a free, uncensored telling of the events in U.S. society and beyond. Second, media professionals and conglomerates have universal access to the public through their various information outlets, newspapers, television shows, and documentary films. Third, current media structures benefit from a corporate structure that allows them to make a profit and thus cross over into entertainment as they share news and information with the general public. This can cause confusion for some media consumers about which information is "real" news and which is soft news or even entertainment. Ultimately, in our fourth component, because of its protection, access, and corporate structure, media outlets are able to construct and support ideologies about the social world as they choose. That is to say, media conglomerates have the power and rights to tell stories as they wish, all the while protecting their profits.

Social scientists also clearly point out that people do not just sit around and wait for the mass media to tell them how and what to think, yet our engagement with events and social phenomena often begins with seeing them on the news or reading about them in a magazine or newspaper. These stories are always already framed for us for our understanding and interest. Our retelling of these stories is influenced by the ways we first encounter them, which makes the mass media quite powerful in our daily lives. As media studies scholars would remind us, the mass media does not reflect reality. Rather, it offers a representation of selected versions of reality. In this way, much of the mass-mediated story telling about sport and physical activity reproduces hierarchies and inequalities in society.

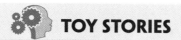 **TOY STORIES**

Compare two sport-related toys (toys with a sport or exercise theme). Your objective is to explore the role of toys in the socialization of children into sport and exercise and in their socialization through sport and exercise.

1. Make observations about the toys and their locations within the store.

   - Name of the toy
   - Recommended age group
   - Price
   - Name of the store
   - Aisle where toy is located (sometimes the aisles are marked: board games, etc.)
   - Other toys (or types of toys) in the vicinity (same aisle, shelf)
   - Describe the packaging (photos, drawings, illustrations, people)

2. Based on these observations, can you tell if the toy is targeted to one particular sex or the other? How do you know?

3. Is the toy sport specific (e.g., mini-golf clubs)? Or is it related more to a physical activity or game (e.g., pogo stick, jump rope)?

4. Are there any indications on the packaging of how kids are supposed to use the toy? In other words, are there suggestions for playing with the toy? This might be indicated with pictures or photos of kids using the toy. The packaging may also include instructions or rules.

5. What might a child learn about the world of sport or exercise (or culture of sport) from using this toy?

6. Would you purchase this toy for your child, niece or nephew, or neighbor? Would you want someone else buying this toy for your child? Why or why not?

7. Does this toy reinforce dominant ideologies (ideas) about gender, race, ethnicity, or ability? Does this toy challenge dominant ideologies about gender, race, ethnicity, or ability?

8. Does this toy reinforce dominant ideologies (ideas) about sport in general (e.g., competition, cooperation, winning, sportsmanship, aggression, skill)? Or about a particular sport (e.g., dunking in basketball)? Does this toy challenge dominant ideologies about sport?

Please note that this is not a finite list of questions that you can ask about your toys. These suggestions aim to get you thinking about how this particular toy might be used, by whom, and why.

This activity originated with sport scholar Dr. Shelley Lucas at Boise State University and is used here with her permission. We think it's a terrific exercise in examining the various ways children (often at very young ages) and their parents are socialized through everyday objects of play.

Sport and the mass media interconnect on a regular and widely observable scale. Sport depends on the media to produce news and information that leads to further commercial opportunities to create stories around events and people that maintain an audience, and in terms of television, to produce broadcasting rights fees as predictable sources of income for promoters and team owners. At the same time, the mass media depends on sport to offer dramatic programming that will continually draw an audience, especially since the advent of television. To continue with our Olympic examples, the amount the IOC can charge for the right to broadcast the Summer Games has gone from just under $.5 million in 1960 to $1.2 billion in 2012. As well, in 2008, the Beijing Olympic Organizing Committee offered press credentials to 4,500 journalists and 1,100 photographers (Coakley, 2009). In these two examples, we see the IOC benefitting from a sure profit (broadcast rights fees) and we see a nation using their hosting of the Olympic Games to bring global media attention to the Games and to their nation's elevated stature through hosting the games.

Sport, Physical Activity, and Religion

Religion is a major sphere of social life that is meant to offer members of society ways to mark and observe transcendent moments in life, such as birth and death, as well as seasonal rituals. Social scientists are not interested in identifying which religions are "best" or matter most to people, but rather how religious practice is part of how people make sense and meaning of everyday life. The social hierarchy of religious practice is also intriguing to social scientists. For example, the social power of Christianity in the United States, including public secular celebrations of Christian holidays (Christmas and Easter), and prayer in schools (which typically means Christian prayer), is a common subject of analysis. The role of religion in the structural and cultural evolution of social systems is also of interest to social scientists, especially as this presence becomes both a stabilizing and contentious point of human interactions.

Religion relies on sport for ritual activities that engage followers in particular body projects that reflect the beliefs underlying the particular religious practice. Sport, in turn, relies on religion to create meaning around sport as a space of transcendence. It is more challenging to return to our Olympic Games example here, but the IOC clearly depends on religious leaders and religious tenets of human goodwill to aid in the two-week break in political and violent aggression during the Games. As well, religious communities depend on global sport events like the Olympics to demonstrate their commonality. Recall the 2012 London Games that became known as the Games of the woman and for some the Games of the Muslim woman.

 Quick Fact

For the first time in the modern Olympic era, three Muslim countries—Brunei, Qatar, and Saudi Arabia—sent women as part of their athlete delegations for the 2012 Summer Games (Smith & Wrynn, 2012). In 2014, the IOC voted to require all host countries to agree to nondiscrimination policies, including gender and religion.

The Short of It

- The major spheres of social life are an organized interrelated set of normative elements that guide behavior of members of society, helping them to define and follow norms, values, and role expectations.

- Functionalist theorists argue that major social institutions contribute to the maintenance and functioning of the entire social system.

- Conflict theorists argue that there are always two classes competing for limited resources. The six major spheres of social life represent a social system that works for some and not for others.

- The sociological concept of socialization refers to a complicated process of transmitting norms, values, and beliefs to society's members. This transmission is accomplished through the structure of major spheres of social life and individual human interactions within those spheres.

- The typically recognized major spheres of life that regularly influence participation in and ideas about sport and physical activity are the economy, education, mass media, religion, family, and politics.

CHAPTER

Body Projects in Sport and Physical Activity

In this chapter you will learn the following:

✓ Sociological framings of the body
✓ Concepts of normalization, regulation, and schooling
✓ Common practices of disciplining bodies in sport and physical activity settings
✓ The role of science and medicine in regulating bodies
✓ The role of mass media in regulating bodies

> A body is a place/location from and through which a person knows and speaks.
>
> **Alexandra Howson and David Inglis (2001)**

Many readers of this book may be too young to recall a sci-fi movie titled *Invasion of the Body Snatchers*. Although not as technically startling and gory as movies may be today, the 1978 film was scary in its ideas about the vulnerability of our bodies to external or alien forces. Playing off of this notion of pods arriving from another life system to take our human life force, scholar Mary Duquin (1994) wrote a timely cautionary note aimed at coaches and scholars working in elite sport and physical activity programs. She warned that our approaches to elite performance may be a new form of body snatchers. Applying her sociological imagination, Duquin suggested that social life, including physical activity and health, was becoming so externally organized by institutions of medicine, health, and private gyms that even our own personal body projects of lifelong physical activity were becoming tightly tied to **normalizing** performance outcomes. She believed that this process was producing citizens who were disassociating from their own unique **embodiment**. Dr. Duquin was not the only scholar talking about bodies and embodiment, but she was one of the first in kinesiology to acknowledge the ways that bodies were becoming dehumanized tools in the projects of elite physical performance.

In concert with Dr. Duquin were many social science scholars studying both societal-level and personal experiential-level components of embodiment. Current understandings of embodied experience took shape in a broad intellectual moment referred to as the **age of science** (mid-1600s to late 1700s). In the context of a capitalist society, these understandings increasingly organized around the profit needs of multinational corporations. For sociologists of sport and physical activity, Dr. Duquin and others were identifying the need to better understand how people and communities live their bodies under these new social conditions.

These scholars were by no means the first to ponder the body or embodiment, an experience and performance of one's body projects in everyday life and varied cultural spaces. Bodies and embodiment did not become important in the modern age. Much early modern anthropological work examined the role of bodies in religious ritual, rites of passage, basic communication, and representation of cultural values. In fact, although it is commonly held that women were historically excluded from sport and physical activities that were not related to the labors of daily life, this is an inaccurate accounting of histories. For example, anthropologists have identified and preserved premodern mosaics indicating a fascination with the role of bodies, embodiment, and physical activity in cultural rituals and daily life and showing women in sporting competitions (e.g., **Sicily's Bikini mosaic**).

Many more examples of the role of bodies and embodiment in daily social life exist, and some are described in the remainder of this chapter. At this point in your developing sociological imagination, you are invited to consider just what a body is; how bodies matter in sport, exercise, and schooling spaces; and the ways bodies are governed, regulated, and sometimes liberated through societal structures and culturally dominant values. In this chapter, we describe and explain the importance of a sociological understanding of the body, embodiment, and the role of sport and physical activity in our cultural constructions of both. As well, we describe the role of sport, physical education, and exercise settings in producing particular types of body ideals and consider the power of mass-mediated representations of bodies in these settings.

The Physical Body as Cultural Artifact

Although all of us have bodies and *live* our bodies every day—that is, we experience life through our bodies, through the ways they interact with the people, places, and things that we encounter throughout our days—we probably do not spend much time thinking about them unless they are causing us difficulty. Bryan Turner suggested in a 1984 work that we experience three different orientations to our bodies: "having a body, doing a body, and being a body" (cited in Moore & Kosut, 2010, p. 2). Some sociologists refer to this daily experience of our embodiment as **physical culture**, or a popular focus on health and trends in bodily aesthetics. Others refer to it as **somatic knowledge**, or one's holistic, embodied interaction in the social world. Others prefer to simply describe bodies as **socially constructed**, meaning they are produced or given meaning through social interaction and context.

No matter what the analytic framing, Chris Shilling (2008) argued that the body is too important to leave in the hands of the natural sciences, for risk of missing

normalizing—A social process of learning and choosing to present one's self and to interact with others in ways that fit with dominant social preferences of the space and time.

embodiment—The ways that social conditions flow through, and are observable through, one's bodily presentation, carriage, and interaction.

age of science—Beyond the timeline, a historical period when human beings were realizing that everyday humans could know about their social, physical, and psychic worlds. Until this time, history suggests, only gods and religious clergy were accepted as "knowers."

Sicily's Bikini mosaic—A historic mosaic depicting social life, perhaps mythology, in a UNESCO World Heritage Site that also depicts luxurious living conditions at the Villa Romana del Casale (in Sicily), the center of the large estate on which the rural economy of the Roman Empire was based.

physical culture—A popular focus on health and trends in bodily aesthetics.

somatic knowledge—One's holistic, embodied interaction in the social world.

socially constructed bodies—Understanding of bodies not merely as physical but as culturally produced (given meaning through social interaction and context).

PAIN AND IDENTITY IN *THE CRASH REEL*

The documentary *The Crash Reel*, released in 2013, documents the career of American snowboarder Kevin Pearce. Pearce, a favorite to represent the United States at the 2010 Vancouver Winter Games and a rival of X-Games and Olympic medalist Shaun White, suffered a traumatic brain injury (TBI) as the result of a fall during a training run leading up the 2010 Games. Director Lucy Walker's film uses footage taken by Pearce, his family and friends, and the media to illustrate his rise in the ranks of snowboarding. Walker documents the process of recovery following the injury for Pearce and his family, as well as the responses and reactions of his friends and competitors, using clips and interviews that show the slow and painful recovery from TBI. Without spoiling the film, Pearce is adamant about his return to the sport that he loves—one that provides so much of his identity—despite his family's misgivings and his doctor's orders to not return to the sport.

How would you feel if you could no longer participate in the activity that provided your central identity and that you loved doing?

the varied social knowledge that emanates from and relies on bodies. In fact, many sociologists find it intriguing to ponder how we might understand bodies in societies as well as society in bodies. Some may go as far as to ask if there really is such a thing as a *natural* body. Think about it—have you ever encountered a person and not already known something about them simply by observing how the person is in his or her body? Does anyone have an innocent, natural body that is unmarked by culture? You may think of a newborn baby, but imagine the full context of the newborn. Is this body only natural, or has it been marked already by cultural norms and values? How do we know this when we see it? This commonplace example points to the analytic bridges that sociologists attempt to create to understand how the so-called natural body is always already a cultural body.

material body—The body in its physical, measurable functions.

role—One's formal position in a social group, such as team captain, brother, coach, umpire, or mentor.

status—One's informal position as related to others in the same social group or in society at large.

activities of daily living—Basic, often personal care activities that human beings typically engage in to perform their daily tasks (e.g., bathing, waste elimination, grocery shopping, cooking, eating).

You may recall that sociologists of sport and physical activity are always concerned with insight and understanding of both structural and cultural aspects of society and social relations. This interest remains the same when considering the body; in fact, the body may be seen as the ultimate social entity in which to observe both structure and culture (Moore & Kosut, 2010). Consider how human beings move from crawling to walking and back to needing support with walking again in older age. Of course, this is a simplistically linear and universal depiction of lifelong physical activity. In reality, we all move with various needs of support throughout our lives due to injury, illness, and developmental change. Such changes are observed as material, or as real, tangible types of bodies that exist in the social world. For example,

SPORTING STATUES AND MATERIAL CULTURE

Examples of memorializing important figures and events in local and global contexts are all around us. Often, elite athletes are the subject of public memorials, whether these are statues, murals, street names, or other honorific structures. This sort of memorializing also points to the enduring cultural power of the body, even after death.

1. How are bodies of celebrities remembered and honored in your community or your campus?

2. Look around the physical space and locate a statue of an athlete. Who is this athlete? Is it an athlete you have heard of, or is it an anonymous athlete representing a group of people? How does the body look? Is it muscular, life sized, accurate? What did this person accomplish to be depicted in statue form? Do people gather at this statue? What does the statue mean to people in your community? (Ask people for their views.)

3. If your campus or community doesn't have a statue, consider other ways athletes are remembered. For whom is the gymnasium or stadium named? What process occurred for that space to have the athlete's (or coach's) name on it? Was there disagreement about this process or the selection of the athlete?

when you visit your older relatives, you may realize you are encountering the aging body. If you have ever visited an injured teammate, you are encountering the sick body. At funerals we encounter the dead body. These framings of the body tend to be static and fixed in a life–death binary of bodily function, focusing on the body as a physical entity only. This is the **material body**.

In a different framing, some social scientists focus on the cultural body, or the body that exists merely as an effect of the way we make sense of bodies in our culturally informed thinking (Casper & Currah, 2011). Here, the aging body takes on cultural effects of **role** and **status**. This is not merely a physically aging body but one that belongs to someone's grandfather or a person who may need to stop driving his car or perhaps needs support for **activities of daily living**. The injured body becomes one that is afforded a break from the typical obligations of daily life (such as attending school or work and taking care of others), again altering one's role and status in various social contexts. A body that is dead becomes more than a body that no longer functions physically—it also offers a narrative of life. Stories of how to live and perhaps how not to live one's life often come into focus when a life ends. For example, tennis professional and social activist Arthur Ashe died in 1993, but his legacy lives on in sport and in ideological and economic relation to various struggles for social justice. Even in death, his life came back into focus because it is permanently linked with other prominent people and moments. More recently, the 2014 death of South African president Nelson Mandela brought

apartheid—A rigid, now-defunct policy of segregating and oppressing non-White members of South African society. Although the policy has been dismantled, a legacy of such segregation continues to exist and exert differential life chances for South Africans.

stacking—A pattern of placing athletes in certain player positions based on racial stereotypes.

renewed attention to Ashe's role in the fight against the racist policy of privilege known as **apartheid**.

The person connected with the dead body is also still a consumer in U.S. society, since this passage brings up needs to pay for end-of-life services, provide a medically approved cause of death, and in some cases gift financial resources to selected recipients. This may be the ultimate example of how the body is never merely material—even in death, the body continues to function as a cultural component of social life. This realization has led some social scientists to focus on the body as a cultural production, or an entity that is most important for the way it reflects back to us our dominant cultural beliefs and practices.

To complicate this a bit more, let's consider the pregnant body. What do you think about when you encounter a lone teenage girl who is pregnant? And what are your ideas when encountering a pregnant woman accompanied by her husband and children? Materially, these examples are simply two pregnant bodies, but culturally, they each tell different stories about social life, status, role, access to resources, and life chances. How is your reading of these two pregnant bodies already informed by your sense of seemingly unrelated issues like ideas about childhood, adulthood, family structure, economics, lifestyle, and sexual morals? When the aging body, sick body, or pregnant body makes an appearance in the Chicago Marathon, what are your culturally informed ideas and reactions?

At the U.S. Track and Field Championships in 2014, former Olympian Alysia Montaño ran the 800-meter race when she was eight months pregnant. There was considerable debate in the media and public discourse about whether Montaño should have been allowed to run in the event, even though her doctor had given her permission.

While it may seem bodies are no-nonsense aspects of our daily existence that require little attention from us, applying a sociological imagination suggests there's more going on here. Sport studies scholars Jennifer Hargreaves and Patricia Vertinsky have argued that "we can only understand the body as multidimensional, constantly produced, and in process" (2007, p. 20). In short, the body is more than a shell for organs and more than a machine that gets put in motion by the mind (the natural sciences approach). It is lived experiences that take up varied social positions across time and place. Still, in the field of kinesiology, we are often guilty of reducing the body to its physical and cognitive parts (mind–body split). This means that in all kinds of science, and even in everyday ponderings about bodies, we often separate the functions of the brain from the functions of the body. This mind–body separation

 We can only understand the body as multidimensional, constantly produced, and in process.

Jennifer Hargreaves and Patricia Vertinsky
in *Physical Culture, Power, and the Body*

Quick Fact

Exercising while pregnant can be beneficial. Misunderstandings and social norms around things like increased perspiration and respiration often turn into myths that keep many expectant mothers from healthfully enjoying exercise throughout pregnancy (Scritchfield, 2012). In 2011, Amber Miller gave birth 7 hours after running the entire 26.2-mile (42 km) Chicago Marathon (O'Connor, 2011).

is known as the Cartesian split, named for French mathematician and philosopher René Descartes, who believed the bodies of animals to be machines controlled by the brain. This privileging of the mind over the body became an intellectual point of contention, and the argument continues today.

For example, in everyday life, we often describe human movement, especially athletic performance, as though it happens naturally, or as though it occurs in a realm outside of external, social, political, and cultural influences. Have you heard people in your family or school refer to someone as "a natural athlete" or maybe as "a brain"? Such proclamations are typically meant in a complimentary way, yet they also often falsely locate people's capacities in an either/or framing of the physical versus the intellectual. We can also see the Cartesian split in the color commentary in elite sport, such as college volleyball, where certain positions are considered the "athletic" positions (e.g., hitter) and others are described as the "thinking" positions (e.g., setter). These categories are discussed in studies on racial **stacking**, or a pattern of placing athletes in certain player positions based on racial stereotypes.

For example, you might have heard about the perceived leadership ("thinking") qualities of White quarterbacks or the speed ("athletic") talent of African American defensive backs (for more on stacking, see Eitzen & Furst, 1989; Gonzalez, 2002; Johnson & Johnson, 1995). In the sociological study of human movement, the material versus cultural distinction and the Cartesian split are typically considered false separations. As this chapter illuminates, an understanding of the body as an active, dynamic force shaping our daily lived experience is most productive. Let's take a look at varied ways the body has been explained by social science scholars.

Body as Resource

Chris Shilling (2005) suggested that the body may be historically and culturally observed as the source for sport today. By this, he meant that the instrumental use of the body for our daily existence (e.g., food gathering, hunting, traveling to resources, trade) led to training and proficiency in particular physical activities, and some of these became part of our leisure pursuits. Thus, historically and contextually, sport and physical activity may be considered as constantly emerging from the realm of demands placed on the human body for subsistence. Often, when we read analyses like this, we imagine Neanderthals and Cro-Magnons emerging from their caves to hunt and gather and make the link that these skills led to fun and games that today we call sport. Shilling suggests the process is much more

FALLON FOX, MIXED MARTIAL ARTIST

Fallon Fox is an American fighter in mixed martial arts (MMA) and the first openly transgender competitor in MMA. Fox was born male but says she struggled with gender issues as a child and as a teen believed she was gay. As a result of pressure placed on her by family and cultural expectations, Fox married, fathered a child, and entered the Navy. In 2006, Fox traveled to Thailand and underwent gender reassignment surgery. In 2013, Fox publicly acknowledged her transgender identity after two professional fights. There has been a great deal of debate about the fairness of allowing Fox to compete in the women's division of MMA. UFC champion Ronda Rousey argues that Fox has an unfair advantage due to being born male, and commentators, fight promoters, and fans echo these claims. Since her revelation, Fox has had six fights, with one loss and five wins. Fox's inclusion and exclusion illustrate the challenges faced by transgender athletes as well as the ways that fans, sport organizers, and athletes struggle to determine fairness, equity, and issues of inclusion.

current than this and indicates that sport continues to emerge alongside the daily demands of human embodiment. For example, the emergence of fantasy sport leagues and various gaming systems that invite living room physical activity reflects the modern technologically linked body as the source for new sport and physical activity practices.

Consider how many people in the United States make a living through physical activity. This is difficult to ascertain, but imagine how many people make a living competing as athletes, coaching elite athletes, and teaching exercise, yoga, and sport skills. In each of these cases, the body becomes a tool for work, an income generator. This is what sociologists of sport and physical activity would refer to as a body as resource not merely to the person working but also to those to whom they have economic obligations. Thus, while the body as a tool may be an athlete on the NFL field on Sunday, his body is also a resource to the NFL corporation and its corporate partners as well as those indirect businesses that make a profit because that football-playing body shows up to do its work on that field. See figure 4.1 for an example of how one body can be a resource for multiple spheres.

 Quick Fact

In 2014, approximately 279,100 experts held jobs in the fitness professional field, putting their bodies to work for the exercise benefit of others. You may wish to become one of these experts whose body is a tool for your occupation, allowing you to earn about $35K annually while sweating it out with youth, older adults, elite athletes, or those in rehabilitation (U.S. Department of Labor, 2015).

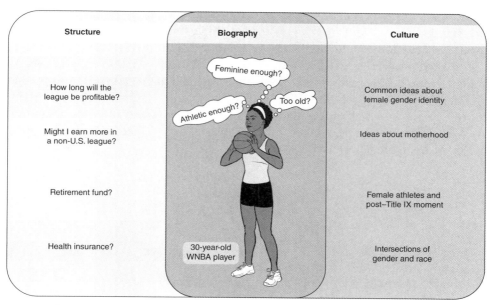

FIGURE 4.1   How might the ideas about biography, structure, and culture change for different bodies described throughout this chapter? Rewrite the image to reflect the external influences on those different types of bodies.

Based on ideas in an illustration by Dr. Yeomi Choi.

Body as Canvas

When we consider the reliance on and uses of the body by medical science and the state, we may observe societal processes and structures playing out on bodies in a project of increasing *rationalization*, or how social scientists refer to the ways the body is required to perform wellness and healthful capacity for the good of the nation. In a simple example, in the United States, a person's driver's license will indicate whether or not they need corrective lenses in order to operate a motor vehicle. In this case, the body is a canvas, or a location for public safety policy. In a more global example, particular parts of the world suffer from infectious disease at different rates than do other locations. In the United States, the Centers for Disease Control and Prevention track rates of infection and origin of these diseases, and then create policy regarding safe travel for U.S. citizens. In conjunction with other state-sponsored agencies, policies such as who may safely donate blood and requirements for immunizations become ways the body is a canvas for medical science and state-sponsored health policy.

In sport and physical activity, your school likely required a physical examination prior to allowing students to participate in team sports. If you remember the early days of schooling, you likely needed to have immunizations before you were allowed to enroll in school. This is an indication that K-12 student bodies are a canvas for a U.S. developed-nation health policy. You may also recall when NBA great Earvin "Magic" Johnson revealed he was HIV positive. The ways his body was managed on and off the court following his diagnosis with the human immunodeficiency virus offer a powerful example of the elite athletic body being used as a location for the application of public health policy, medical science, and state-sponsored sexual morality (Dworkin & Wachs, 2000). Clearly, Magic Johnson remained someone with more resources than many to make cutting-edge health care decisions, yet his body also became instrumental to public policy and his role as professional athlete made this an even more powerful instrumentation. As we have suggested previously, his body was at once a material (physical) and cultural (ideological) canvas.

⌛ TERRY FOX

Terry Fox is one of Canada's national heroes, though many in the United States might not recognize his name. In 1980, Terry Fox embarked on a quest to run across Canada by running the equivalent of a marathon each day to raise money for cancer research. Fox had been diagnosed with cancer and had his

Anonymous/AP/Press Association Images

Terry Fox running in his Marathon of Hope to raise awareness of cancer, while displaying his heroic body.

right leg amputated above the knee. He was running his cross-country trek with a prosthetic limb. Initially, Fox's run failed to generate much media attention, though by the time he reached Ontario, crowds began to line the streets, cheer him on, and donate money. After 143 days and 3,339 miles, Fox had to end his attempt when the cancer returned to his body. He had raised $1.7 million and had also come to signify something about Canadian identity. He died in June 1981.

Fox has been celebrated in a number of ways with awards, a postage stamp, a coin, streets and schools named for him, and eight statues across Canada. Each statue shows a representation of Fox with his prosthetic limb, celebrating his body as heroic. (Only a few statues in the United States represent people with disabilities. President Franklin Roosevelt is depicted in his wheelchair in Washington, D.C., Olympic hammer thrower Harold Connolly is presented in a statue in Massachusetts with his shorter and weaker left arm, and Paralympian Cara Dunne-Yates is remembered with a statue in Snowmass, Colorado.)

One element that makes Fox's accomplishments and the celebrations of those accomplishments perhaps more meaningful is his status as an everyman; he was not a professional athlete, but a person who used movement to raise awareness about a cause. In the process, he became a symbol of his country and its ideals.

Sociologists See Governing Structures for Embodiment and Body Projects

Today, sociology of the body is a growing area of interest in the sociology of sport and physical activity, and it often takes on interests in health and wellness as well. This particular area of study makes room for varied physical activity engagements, including dance; bodybuilding; body size management; disability sport; bodies in gaming; and medical framings of bodies in schools, sport, and exercise. Although sociological interest in the body is not new, it takes on new analytic framings in current intellectual, political, and economic contexts. This means that in a moment where diverse identity categories and myriad choices for personal embodiment are available, the meanings of bodies and embodiment are changing rapidly in terms of time, space, and access to resources.

Not too long ago, people with disabilities might have felt uncomfortable with social display of their embodied difference. Today, many forms of disability are commonly encountered in public spaces. For example, rather than desiring a prosthetic leg that looks like a close match to one's biological leg, a physically active person may prefer a technical leg that displays performance capacity more than a natural human aesthetic. The notion of difference in how bodies work and move is more commonplace today, in part due to technological advances, but also due to an increase in the presence and honoring of injured military veterans. When, in our analyses of bodies, we turn our attention to body projects rather than physical skill and performance, we engage a whole set of social science principles and goals.

Sociologists pay a good deal of attention to the ways that bodies get coerced into particular kinds of embodiment, discipline, management, and progress goals. For example, in the current panic over the obesity epidemic, schools, leisure programs, and governmental organizations are collaborating to increase physical activity among youth and to teach them how to manage their weight as a crucial part of a healthy lifestyle. Burrows and Wright (2004) suggested that we ought to be concerned about the various consequences of a message that one's body is an entity in need of

Quick Fact

Sport England reports that the number of disabled people who take part in sport has risen significantly, but barriers remain. Weekly participation in sport among people over 16 years old with a long-term limiting illness, disability, or infirmity is at 17.2 percent. That's around half of the general population level. Participation varies depending on the type of disability. People with sensory impairments have a much lower participation rate, at just 13.4 percent. Health limitations (74%) were the main barrier for disabled adults, while lack of money and the unsuitability of sports facilities were significant disabling conditions mentioned by disabled young people (37%; Sport England, n.d.).

management or repair, especially among children in school settings. Moreover, they encourage us to ask the following questions: Are there other ways young people ought to be in touch with their bodies? How do such disciplining structures link with others like anti-drug, anti-sex messages that kids receive in schools? How do schools, parents, and broader community structures actually deliver these social and moral lessons?

Consider some recent television shows that focus on the body and the need to fix or correct it. These shows include *The Biggest Loser* and other weight-loss shows as well as shows that focus on plastic surgery and medical alterations to the body. Make no mistake, developing a sociological understanding of bodies is daunting. Therefore, many sociologists of sport and physical activity feel a responsibility to deconstruct previously held notions about bodies and to develop social, cultural, and political literacies around the body that enable us to better advocate for a more physically active world. In fact, applying a sociological imagination to one's thinking about bodies and social conditions may ensure that all bodies are able to engage in meaningful physical activity and that zero bodies are disallowed from physical activity spaces.

Schooling Bodies

Historically, school physical education has had a public health and national defense component to it. That is, school physical education offered an accessible space in which the state could educate citizens about good health practices and instill values for maintaining the practices beyond the schoolyard. K-12 physical education in the United States can be one of the most fun and productive educational spaces that a student can encounter, and it may also be a space of population surveillance and control. Consider fitness testing in your physical education classes. Do you recall learning about the national norms or standards of performance for your age group? Depending on the specific set of fitness tests that your teacher used, you also had a report, like Fitnessgram, sent home that let you and your parents know how your scores relate to **criterion-based health standards** and offered advice for how you could improve or maintain your overall fitness. Learning these skills and understanding one's fitness as part of an overall interest in one's health status are potentially liberating things. At the same time, if this focus on fitness standards shifts our focus from a range of physical activities to engaging in physical activity solely for the purpose of medicalized health-risk reduction, then we see the body snatchers returning. Sociologists would suggest that physical education spaces are also spaces of disciplining bodies and creating obedient or **docile citizens**. Furthermore, sociologists and advocates with a sociological imagination might ask why this medicalized health goal gets more attention and resources than, say, a leisure-oriented discovery goal where students might be introduced physical activities they could enjoy throughout their lives.

criterion-based health standards—Recommended health standards and measures (like number of sit-ups in a fitness test or oxygen uptake during exercise) for various social categories such as age and sex.

docile citizens—Members of society who have adopted the dominant ideas about striving and existing in the social world and thus do not seek to change the system but rather to change their individual selves.

Consider your own experiences in school. In what ways were they teaching you lessons far beyond the textbooks? And to what extent did your embodiment matter in your daily experience of school? Given these insights, what must we all know so that we do not uncritically overdiscipline bodies and thereby possibly contain their uniqueness and creativity in human movement practices? Schools do a lot of governing of bodies, especially at the K-12 level, but also in colleges and universities. For example, the drilling and exercising done in the physical education classroom are meant to teach lessons about authority, rule following, and persistence as much as about choosing a physically active lifestyle. As previously mentioned, the fact that your school likely required immunizations and other records before offering you medical clearance for being present in the school is one more example of the role of schools in disciplining bodies. In other words, the school becomes an extension of public health agendas by not allowing students with possible infectious conditions to set foot on school grounds. Because physical education is also fun at times, sociologists refer to its disciplining components as a looser form of power over the body. However, this fun approach is no less powerful—in fact, it likely allows students and parents to buy in to ideas of individual responsibility for health and wellness while not becoming politically active about the unequal access to health care and physical activity spaces.

The school-based research of Evans, Davies, and Wright (2004) and many other sociologists of sport and physical activity offers examples of the ways physical education and health curricula contribute to social constructions of bodies as well as a historical context for this sort of governance of bodies within educational settings. They proposed that schools focus on "young minds" with bodies, which suggests that school-aged bodies are considered something to manage, not a resource for knowledge acquisition. Children are present but not actively featured in the most important school learning outcome goals. To the extent that schools focus on cultivating young minds and containing young bodies, they are contributing to the Cartesian split discussed earlier and simply ignoring the place of the body in learning capacities. An example of bodies coming into the learning project within school settings is Brain Gym. Unfortunately, schools most often privilege the mind as though it operates separately from the body. With budget cuts to physical education, we also see different ways of delivering information, including online physical

 BODIES IN YOUR SCHOOL

Schools become social spaces where members of society learn their role, status, and the most acceptable ways of being and acting in their own bodies. For example, what to wear; how to move in the classroom, on the playground, and around other kids; and even which bodies are most ideal in size, shape, and ability are all lessons learned at school.

1. What does it feel like to be in your body at your school?

2. How are bodies differentiated by peers, by teachers, and by parents?

education. In what ways do you see students, teachers, coaches, fitness leaders, and other allied professionals policing bodies?

Sporting Bodies

Sport settings are both controlling and liberating for the body. The controlling aspects of sport come in the form of team rules, sport governance, requirements for student-athletes, and health regulation of student-athletes. Liberating aspects may include social status on campus, exploring new sport skills, and, for very few, financial benefit. Examples of state governance of individual bodies may be observed in sporting, schooling, and exercising spaces. In professional sport, bodies are often described as tools for the job, and they are just that at times. One of the questions your sociological imagination might lead you to is what the working conditions are for professional athletes. Often, we romanticize the lives of professional athletes, but our sociological imagination might suggest that these lives are uniquely demanding, especially on the body. If you have a sore muscle from your daily workout, you may use a doctor-prescribed or over-the-counter medication to get some relief. If you are professional athlete, you will not only be expected to perform elite athletic feats, but you will also be more restricted than most people in terms of which substances you may ingest in order to keep your body performing at that level. Your body will be subjected to tests for the presence of illegal or banned substances, which are decided by the sport employer. Moreover, once under contract by a professional team, your body literally becomes equipment for that team. In terms of tax laws, the team owners are allowed to take a tax break called depreciation based on the annual demise of your body due to

 BLACK WOMEN IN SPORT FOUNDATION

The Black Women in Sport Foundation (BWSF) was established in 1992. Tina Sloan Green, Alpha Alexander, PhD, Nikki Franke, PhD, and Linda Greene founded the BWSF as one means to increase the participation of Black girls and women in all aspects of sport, including as athletes, coaches, and sport administrators. The BWSF offers sport programming for boys and girls primarily in the Philadelphia area. Sloan Green currently serves as the president and executive director of the BWSF and has had a storied career in athletics. She participated on the U.S. women's lacrosse team in its early years (1969-1973), as well as on the U.S. women's field hockey team in 1966. Both sports have relatively low numbers of African American participants. Sloan Green served as the head coach for the Temple University women's lacrosse team for 18 years (1973-1992), and she is a member of the Women's Sports Foundation Hall of Fame, the Lacrosse Hall of Fame, and the halls of fame at Temple and West Chester Universities. Although African American female athletes are represented in basketball and track and field, they are still underrepresented in all other sports and in the coaching ranks. The BWSF is one organization determined to increase these numbers.

the demands of your sport labor. Typically, depreciation is taken on things like the delivery van for a flower shop, but in professional sports, this tax law may also be applied to human bodies.

culture of risk—A dominant cultural acceptance of injury risk in sport involvement.

Most obvious in sport settings is what some scholars refer to as the **culture of risk**, or a dominant cultural acceptance of injury risk in sport involvement. The accepted level of risk increases with the increasing level of performance—thus, the most elite performers are expected to "gut it out," "take one for the team," or "push through the pain." In support of this culture of risk, U.S. colleges and universities prepare and supply a team of first responders, or sports medicine professionals whose main duties are to respond to acute injuries occurring during a sport contest. More recently, sports medicine professionals in the United States have become more integral to debates about athlete health and wellness, especially in light of news about the rate of concussions and brain injury in the NFL and other contact sport settings. Even as these first responders provide vital resource to athletes, their work is also part of the governance of elite sporting bodies.

Exercising Bodies

The reasons for and types of engagement in exercise change over time in all societies, from health benefits to preferred beauty standards to functional movement (transportation, leisure, social). Sociologists of sport and physical activity are most interested in dominant values influencing exercise access and involvement. It is also important for social scientists to understand how something like daily exercise became so prominent and even morally expected of good citizens. That is, what are the various external influences that shape involvement in exercise, including choices for exercise, time for exercise, and support for exercise? One current example of the dominant moral imperative to exercise is the growing global fear of fat. The occurrence of obesity, which indicates that a person has excess body fat (not body weight, but particularly body fat), has spawned a host of medical, social, political, and entertainment responses.

Sociologists of sport and physical activity might ask whether the science and media around the issues of overweight and obesity are somehow invested in particular forms of dominance. Which bodies are normative? How are they marked as such? What are the structures that reinforce the normalizing of particular bodies (e.g., laws, policies, local taste, expert knowledge)? Many scholars prefer to talk about somatic selves, embodiment, body image, and the social construction of fat. For example, Pirkko Markula (1995) studied participants in aerobics exercise classes and tried to understand what was at the core of their desire to participate in this form of exercise. She found it was not merely joy or external messages about personal obligation to exercise that motivated these particular women, but perhaps some combination of both. Even what these women described as their very own desire to exercise was already informed by external messages about personal health, body size, and looking good. In this sort of sociological analysis, Markula's work enhances our understanding of the structural and cultural contours of physical activity involvement and helps us to see the complex nature of how we make personal choices in the midst of social conditions.

Out-of-Sync Bodies

The U.S. fitness movement has many origins, but perhaps three things can be brought to light as key components of this movement. First was the advent of television programming that included exercise, allowing the bodybuilder and health enthusiast subcultures to develop a broader audience through broadcasts like *The Jack LaLanne Show* in the 1950s. Second was the brilliant accessibility of the health-related research from the Cooper Institute. While there had been research studies indicating that exercise was good for human health, it was not until the Cooper Institute put this information into an easily understandable set of standards, goals, and outcomes that everyday people took an interest. Although their research began as a way to support astronauts in training their bodies to withstand the demands of atmospheric changes, they eventually translated these exercise regimens to common citizens. When Cooper published his 1964 book, titled simply *Aerobics*, he invited common citizens to train like astronauts to reduce health risk and extend their life spans. The availability and accessibility of this cutting-edge knowledge marked a trend in exercise as preventive personal health care and significantly influenced an American fitness movement. Ask someone born before 1970 about this—they will likely recall a moment when it seemed like people began running or walking for health benefits. This is also the time when the **surgeon general** of the United States indicated a formula for exercise-related health benefits. This national interest in fitness and health-related physical activity also opened the door to the third component, consumerism and the production of exercise experts. It is hard to imagine anyone but Nike producing the most popular exercise gear, but at the height of the U.S. fitness movement, the Reebok aerobic shoe was the must-have social status marker. It was also in this moment that corporate fitness programs took shape and fitness plans and gyms became a common benefit to full-time employment. Private fitness facilities also grew in this moment and still exist today, especially since the equipment in these spaces is too big for home use.

From fitness we move to fatness. Many sociologists of sport and physical activity are turning their attention to popular ideas and medicalized information regarding body size. Surely you are aware of the so-called obesity epidemic. For social scientists, this fear of fat raises sociological questions about trends in body size throughout history and ideals of beauty, discrimination, and structural issues related to changing human relationships to food and physical activity. For example, in their book *Food Fight*, Dr. Kelly Brownell and K.B. Horgen (2004) describe the changes in the American landscape, food production, and resources for physical activity to offer a holistic approach to understanding changes in human body size and health.

surgeon general—The operational head of the U.S. Public Health Service Commissioned Corps and, by virtue of this position, the leading spokesperson on matters of public health in the United States.

Social scientists suggest that "fat bodies" are indeed always in process and are subject to the dominant ideas circulating around them in any given politicohistorical moment. Herndon (2002) suggested that in the absence of a standard for defining what is fat in Western society, an impression of cultural fatness gets imposed to stigmatize people, especially women, marking them not only as fat but also immoral. Echoing this, Longhurst (2005) argued

WEIGHING IN ON *THE BIGGEST LOSER*

The Biggest Loser is a reality television show that first aired in the United States in 2004. It has since celebrated 17 seasons and expanded to more than 20 countries. The premise of the show is a competition among overweight contestants to lose weight; the contestant who loses the highest percentage of starting weight is determined to be "the biggest loser" and wins $1 million. *The Biggest Loser* is affiliated several products and advertisers and has expanded its products to include videos, cookbooks, video games, race series, fat camp, and other online components. To enhance its entertainment value, the show ups the drama of weight loss and exercise by tempting the contestants with favorite foods and putting them through physical fitness challenges as well as pitting contestants against one another. All this does not always create the healthiest environment in which to lose weight. Moreover, the show chooses contestants to represent a range of identities, including gender, racial, ethnic, and age variations. Amid accusations of various unhealthy training principles, mistreatment of contestants, and concerns about unrealistic messaging to viewers, the popularity of the show has spawned other similar shows, including *Heavy*, *I Used to Be Fat*, *Extreme Weight Loss*, *Shedding for the Wedding*, *Celebrity Fit Club*, and *Thintervention with Jackie Warner*.

Weight loss should be done in a healthy, balanced manner through moderate exercise and healthy eating habits that can be maintained for a lifetime.

that the word *fat* is in the very least incendiary and at its core may be a spoken or rhetorical violence in Western society, especially because it typically refers to an "immoral dirty-ness" or "a moral and physical decay" (p. 249). In elite sport, professional golfers John Daly and Laura Davies live in bodies that trouble the boundaries of nature and culture, especially since they are considered fat athletes

(Jamieson, Stringer, & Andrews, 2008). To the extent these bodies resist technologies of healthism, or medicalized framings of individual responsibility for the absence of health risks in one's body, they illuminate the frailty of overdetermined medical models that attempt to predict health outcomes. That is, their athletic excellence and productivity may be a rupturing point in an otherwise tightly knit story about the fall of Western society due to lack of physical activity and increasing collective fatness (Gard & Wright, 2006). What if we could all be fat *and* successful *and* healthy? Would we tune in to watch a show called *The Biggest Winner* where fat, successful people tell us their stories? Or does the phrase the biggest loser offer life lessons that fit better with our belief in our competitive, individualistic, success-oriented society? Consider the dual roles of fitness and fatness in your own experiences in sport and physical activity and try to imagine these as more than personal troubles but rather social issues.

To the extent that elite athletes who are fat take up new subject positions, they may also disrupt medicalized knowledge of fatness and ultimately open up new analytic spaces for interrogation of when, how, and why body size matters (Gremillion, 2005). At the very least, analyses like that of golfers Daly and Davies raise critical questions about how size matters, what kinds of bodies are athletic bodies, how fatness resonates with other hierarchies of bodies, and in what ways sport opens up or closes down particular bodily ways of being. Anyone interested in developing a sociological perspective on sport and physical activity must heed Helen Gremillion's (2005) call to everyday analytic action: "When body size matters, the cultural politics of understanding why matters as well" (p. 26).

Mass-Mediated Bodies

It is generally accepted that the mass media constructs and reconstructs cultural events in particular ways and for a variety of purposes (Birrell & Cole, 1994; Duncan, 1994; Kane & Greendorfer, 1994). Although the power of the media is pervasive in its television, radio, print, and electronic options, consumers—real people—make their own meaning of the texts they engage with. Sport is a common site for the production of mediated images, but curiously, sport industry texts have seldom been examined regarding the varied meanings they may be constructing about specific sporting bodies (Buysse & Embser-Herbert, 2004). McDonald and Birrell (1999) advanced the use of cultural studies frameworks for identifying larger cultural meaning in particular sporting events and personalities, and they articulated precisely how this work ought to be done. First, the authors suggested that "narratives are the means through which particular incidents are given meaning by particular producers" (p. 293). Also key to reading sport critically is historicizing narratives. This means that any counternarrative articulates what the event means in the particular historical moment rather than laying claim to a master narrative that would be presumed true across time and space. Ultimately, "reading sport critically" suggests that narratives must be considered for the important ideological work that they do and that counternarratives be seen for their unique work in "offering resistant visions while creating spaces for the mobilization of political action" (McDonald & Birrell, 1999, p. 295). In this collection, critical cultural analyses of MLB pitcher Nolan Ryan,

LPGA golfer Nancy Lopez, NBA player Earvin "Magic" Johnson, and figure skater Tonya Harding are offered as models of reading sport for its role in producing and contesting dominant social ideas around gender, race, social class, and sexuality.

Superhuman Bodies: Physically Active Bodies and Technology

American fans seem to simultaneously desire a purity to sport and superhuman feats of athleticism and fitness. In the current day, most people, from leisure walkers to elite performers, rely on some sort of technology to track their physical activity engagement and performance, such as Fitbit, free fitness apps, and GPS gadgets. Yet, in recalling the preceding governing structures and disabling conditions, there remain several examples in sport and physical activity where bodies that move or work differently are effectively disallowed from particular activity spaces. To the extent that we have learned to relate to our bodies as machines—machines that we need to keep in good, working order—many of us increasingly rely on technology for help. Tiger Woods had LASIK surgery to enhance his vision—a physical enhancement that surely increased the likelihood of success as a professional golfer. This enhancement is considered legal under the rules of golf, but other uses of technology are not (e.g., binoculars for sighting), yet the technology exists to enhance one's vision beyond 20/20. So the question remains—is Tiger Woods' surgically enhanced vision an unfair advantage? More recently, German long jumper Markus Rehm won the German National Championships, making him eligible for the European Championships. However, Rehm competes using a prosthetic leg. Because of this technological "advantage," the German track and field federation decided to not allow him to represent Germany in the European Championships. Is competing with a prosthetic leg an unfair advantage?

The Short of It

- Sociology of the body is a growing interest area in the sociology of sport and physical activity. It includes research on varied physical activity engagements, such as dance; bodybuilding; body size management; disability sport; bodies in gaming; and medical framings of bodies in schools, sport, and exercise.

- Sociologists turn their attention to body projects, rather than to physical skill and performance, in order to engage a whole set of social science principles and goals.

- Bodies are both physical and cultural entities at all times. Sociologists suggest that we experience three orientations to our bodies "having a body, doing a body, and being a body" (Turner cited in Moore & Kosut, 2010, p. 2).

- Bodies are socially constructed through interactions in various sporting, exercising, and schooling spaces.

CHAPTER 5

Diversity, Difference, and Power in Sport and Physical Activity

In this chapter you will learn the following:

✓ Distinguishing between social stratification and inequality
✓ How sociologists define and study power
✓ Existing patterns of stratification and inequality in sport, physical education, and exercise settings
✓ The role of sport and physical activity in addressing social inequalities
✓ How diversity, difference, and power show up in physical activity settings

> Activities, spaces and equipment are heavily gender-typed: Playgrounds, in short, have a [somewhat] fixed geography of gender.
>
> **Barrie Thorne** in *Gender Play: Girls and Boys in School*

By now you have been encouraged to enhance your sociological imagination through pondering major spheres of life and the importance of bodies in everyday social interactions. In this chapter, we invite you to consider the forms of diversity, social power, and inequalities that may be observed in sporting, exercising, and schooling spaces. Consider your favorite professional sport team. Look at the roster and see where the players are from. There may be different patterns of representation in different sports and in different regions of the world. You may also consider the Olympic Games and the difference in the ways that nations dominate from the Summer Games to the Winter Games. How do we make sense of this?

A good starting point here may be to think about your own experiences in sport and physical activity. Consider whether or not you felt a commonality with your peers. Or perhaps you had feelings of being different from everyone else. Sociologists are interested in the structural and cultural conditions that produce such varied patterns of involvement in sport and physical activity at all levels.

More locally, think about your school and parks where people exercise or engage in leisure-time physical activity. Ask people older than you if the representation of people in these physical activity spaces has changed over time. Chances are that things have changed in the patterns of gender, age, ability, race, and social class in these community spaces. This sort of change is natural in all societal spaces—people come and go in ways that are tied to changing societal structures, like those major spheres of influence from chapter 3. For example, when a new Hebrew Academy opens in a community, one's Jewish classmates in public school may diminish, and interactions between Jewish youth and youth of other religions may change a bit due to this new opportunity. Again, such changes in communities are common and become entangled with historic and current local and global ideas about difference. Our focus in this chapter is social difference, or diversity, and societal power associated with such differences, especially as these take shape in sporting, exercising, and schooling spaces.

Sport, Physical Activity, and Social Stratification

For sociologists, it is clear that all societies are stratified. **Stratification** is a social process of distribution of resources, often in ways that share these resources inequitably. Despite common beliefs to the contrary, U.S. society operates as a class system. In general, our dominant societal-level belief in rewards for hard work, or **meritocracy**, leads us to disbelieve our organizational structure as a hierarchical and potentially uneven class system. Yet, look around your daily environments—it is easy to identify evidence of stratification, such as educational attainment, place of residence and settlement, workforce involvement, school sport and physical education involvement, professional sport spectatorship, and leisure-time pursuits. That is, the makeup of people in any societal space reflects a historical legacy of human movement, sharing of ideas, merging of languages, and of course different access to power in determining which social difference matters as well as how that social difference matters.

One might imagine that sport and physical activity are fair and open spaces where social difference, elitism, and power are irrelevant—the epitome of the level playing field. That would be a limited perspective on the power of sport as an important cultural space that both relies on and challenges social difference. In the broad field of kinesiology, those who study sociology of sport and physical activity have focused their analytic attention on issues of *access*, *atmosphere*, *governance*, and *control*. The primary categories of social difference under analysis have been race, social class, gender, and more recently sexuality and disability. While these categories of social difference are powerful on their own, it is important to understand that they gain cultural power through their constant interaction.

Sociologically focused kinesiologists also stress the importance of understanding positions of privilege as well as those of disadvantage in all social hierarchies. Some refer to this as studying across difference or studying up. The critical point here is the recognition that social difference is natural and ever present; the social hierarchies attached to this social difference are not natural. Hierarchies are created by people, or socially constructed, rather than based on any sort of evidence. More specifically, sport and physical activity research indicates patterns of differential rates of access, participation, and control across social categories of race, social class, gender, sexuality, and ability. These are issues of representation, and they are often considered crucial structural issues in the overall systems of sporting, exercising, and schooling spaces. So, when you look around your own sport team roster and you wonder why nobody else looks, moves, or talks like you, you have an opportunity to apply your sociological imagination and to go beyond personal experience to think about the structural and cultural conditions that made such social stratification possible.

Directly related to social stratification is social hierarchy, or, as many scholars have called it, the difference that difference makes. This concept is both simple and complex for

stratification—The various ways resources (e.g., finances, time) are distributed.

meritocracy—The belief that ability will determine outcome, as expressed through the novels of Horatio Alger, who wrote after the Civil War about characters who pulled themselves up by their bootstraps and overcame their low social class standing to become successful.

NAMES, LOGOS, AND MASCOTS

Eitzen and Baca Zinn (1989) examined the names, logos, and mascots for 1,185 four-year colleges. They found that more than half the schools employed names that are sexist and demean women. Schools located in the American South were more likely to have sexist names for their women's athletic teams. Examples of such names are the Lady Rams, the Teddy Bears, and the Pink Panthers. The authors concluded that these names of athletic teams reinforce sport as a masculine space.

1. What changes have schools made in the gender marking of their team names since Eitzen and Baca Zinn collected their data?

2. Think about your high school and college mascots and the teams you play in your conference. Do any of these schools have team names or mascots that are gender marked?

3. Can you identify other forms of gender marking in the world of sport?

social scientists, and it takes on unique complications in sport and physical activity. In its most simple form, the concept recognizes that members of society have arbitrarily assigned value to social difference. This has created a social hierarchy that would otherwise not naturally be present. A sport-specific example is the belief that biologically male bodies are more suited to elite athleticism than are biologically female bodies. Rules, guidelines, and the organizational structure of most physical activity programs are organized around this concept of naturalized gender difference. Beliefs about natural racial superiority in certain sports are another example, such as the widespread belief that Kenyan runners are naturally gifted, which fails to recognize training techniques that may account for their long-distance running success.

In another example, Dr. Mary Louise Adams (2011) highlighted the role of sport in reflecting and informing current beliefs about difference as she described the historical shift of men's involvement in the sport of figure skating. At one time, figure skating was seen as a gentleman's sport. Over time the image of the sport was of primarily effeminate male involvement, which was highlighted in the 1990s when a group of skaters put new effort into performing a more preferred masculinized version of figure skating. Studying men's figure skating throughout the 20th century

The specific upper-class masculinity that shaped 19th-century English figure skating stemmed from a racialized world view that saw elegant activities like skating as symbols of "civilized society" and idealized community of interests that was seen as the exclusive domain of privileged white Europeans.

Mary Louise Adams in *Artistic Impressions: Figure Skating, Masculinity, and the Limits of Sport*

raises many questions about the naturalness of categories of difference and the ways that major social spheres, including sport and physical activity, play crucial roles in reflecting and even creating such ideas about difference.

Beyond this naming of the human creation of social hierarchies lies another level of understanding that is more deeply contextualized, or reflective of culturally specific values and beliefs. Differences exist within groups as well as between groups. Not to be confusing, but *these differences matter differently in different sporting spaces*. For example, when Oscar Pistorius, who'd had both legs amputated below the knee, competed in both the London Paralympics and the Olympic Games in 2012, his belonging in each of these sporting locations became contested. According to the critics, one is either a Paralympian or a "real" Olympian. (What do you think?) Moreover, the culture of elite sport to which Pistorius belongs places him in a position of privilege in relation to most people, especially those who live with disability and may not easily gain access to sport. He is also a White South African man. Each of these social categories (race, gender, nation, and class) interrelate to situate Pistorius in ways that make his disability matter differently than that of a working-class Black South African woman who is not running for the nation. The work of Adams (2011) and others also offers evidence to complicate the all-too-common two-way (binary) categories of difference.

In another example, Mark Bingham was an amateur elite rugby athlete and an openly gay man. Sociologists of sport and physical activity examine the role of sport, coupled with his heroic involvement in the rerouting of United Airlines flight 93 (hijacked on September 11, 2001), in making his particular presentation of gay masculinity allowable in a society that most often prefers either/or categories of difference (King, 2009). In some ways, this concept is simple (the meaning of difference is created by people); in other ways, it is incredibly complex (the difference that difference makes is historicized and deeply contextual).

 ## RACIAL CODING OF SPORTSMANSHIP

Simons (2003) examined the NCAA's sportsmanship policies and contended that African American football and basketball players are penalized at a greater rate than their teammates and opponents. Penalized behaviors involve verbal and nonverbal behaviors, including dancing in the end zone, trash talking, and celebrating a dunk. Simons critiqued the sportsmanship policies, placing them in an elitist amateur sport culture, but also considered the participation rates of African American men in football and basketball and the use of the sportsmanship policy to control athletes of color. A funny *Key & Peele* skit where Hingle McCringleberry is penalized for his end-zone celebrations illustrates this phenomenon (www.comedycentral.com/video-clips/obd3jl/key-and-peele-mccringleberry-s-excessive-celebration).

If scoring is an important element of sport competitions, why are sport leagues interested in punishing celebrations?

Systems of Power Are Not Individual Identities

Scholars have studied difference for years. Some of the frameworks applied to the study of difference have blamed victims of institutionalized hierarchies for their own problems (e.g., deficiency models, assimilationist models), and others have attempted to understand social stratification as a phenomenon of all societies based on dominant beliefs and ruling cultural norms. For example, when the lack of U.S. Latinas in college is explained as a deficiency of Latino families (e.g., a hypermasculine style of child rearing and lack of value of education), this is a deficiency model explanation. Suggesting that all Latino families are deficient fails to recognize related structural factors that may also explain the low college enrollment among Latinas. In fact, research indicates that family and household income, parent education level, systematic tracking of working-class students into non-college curricula, and lack of institutional insiders may all have something to do with the rate of college enrollment. Examining all of these external forces is a more complicated, more accurate explanation of the many social forces that influence something like rate of college enrollment and rate of physical activity participation.

To identify as a Mexican-American woman and to know one's own experiences of race, social class, gender, and sexuality are of course important, but individual identity and experience are not equivalent to a sociological understanding of the ways that societies become systematically stratified across axes of difference. In other places around the world, the differences Americans take for granted between men and women or between racial groups may not even be relevant. Of course, how we as people come to self-identify is greatly influenced by the categories of difference deemed important by a dominant culture. Thus, identities and systems of power are interrelated, but they are very different representations of stratification in a society. Systems of power represent the systemic meaning assigned to categories of difference, influencing how members of society interact and access resources. Typically, categories of race, social class, gender, sexuality, and physicality are understood as social organizing principles—that is, they are something you live, not an identity you have. Consider social categories as organizing principles that shape access, atmosphere, and governance and control in and through sport and physical activity settings.

Sociologists spend a good amount of time trying to understand the ways that everyday people gain **access** to social spaces, exercise power in those spaces, and control what happens in those spaces. We can think of access in terms of participation rates in sport and physical activity, especially across the life span. Patronage is related to access, but it is different because people must first have access to particular social spaces and social groups in order to choose to regularly participate. For sociologists, patronage refers to rates of participation and support of particular sport, exercise, and schooling spaces. A person who has not learned to swim is unlikely to take up outrigger canoeing, and an adult who never learned to lift weights in K-12

access—The ability of a member of society to gain entry to and fully participate in a particular social space. This does not refer only to economic access, although it is crucial.

atmosphere—A complicated interaction of social norms, ideas about identity categories, and what it feels like to interact in a particular social space.

BLACK QUARTERBACKS

Before American colleges and universities integrated, Black football players routinely filled the position of quarterback at Black high schools and historically Black colleges and universities (HBCU). As schools became integrated, the position came to be identified with certain character traits—such as leadership, good decision making, coolness under pressure, and intelligence—that most White coaches considered to be more present in White players, cementing the Whiteness of the position. Similarly, these coaches considered Black players to be fast and assigned them to positions that relied on speed, such as running back, wide receiver, and corner backs. These stereotypes, based on outdated racist ideas around skills being connected to genetics, have been hard to let go. The first Black quarterback to start in the Super Bowl was Doug Williams in Super Bowl XXII in January 1988. In 2013, the NFL season opened with nine starting Black quarterbacks. With the increase of Black quarterbacks in the collegiate ranks and NFL, we might wonder when we should expect to see other racial and ethnic groups represented at the central position.

© Carlos Gonzalez/Minneapolis Star Tribune/ZumaPress.com

African American football players like Vikings quarterback Teddy Bridgewater are finally being utilized in leadership positions on the field.

PE is less likely to take up CrossFit. In each of these examples, these people may have access points to these physical activity spaces, but they lack the life chances to make it likely that they will regularly participate in or even support (financially or otherwise) these activities.

Atmosphere is a complicated interaction of social norms, ideas about identity categories, and what it feels like to interact in a particular social space. For example, have you ever been the only girl in the free-weight room or the youngest person on your summer league team? The feeling of belonging or sometimes of crossing boundaries is an expression of the social and cultural power in the social space. It's not a "push you out of the way" kind of power but a more subtle, ever-present ambience or feeling within the space that reflects dominant or ruling beliefs about all kinds of difference, such as race, social class, gender, sexuality, and ability (Douglas, 2002).

Related to both access and atmosphere, **governance** and **control** of sporting spaces are typically studied as a kind of formal authority to decide who gets access and which forms of cultural power will matter most in the space. In sport, we often think of team owners as those with the most control over the professional sport setting. This would be very different in leisure and exercise settings, which are diversely structured social spaces. Certainly, gym owners and club members might have control over the organization and accessibility of the space. When we think about physical education, we think about teachers as having control, but we might also suggest that parents, principals, and even politicians may exercise control over physical education.

Social Conditions Versus Individual Identities

For sociologists, each member of society enters the world inheriting a set of social conditions, and daily life is a process of interacting in relation to those conditions. The section that follows should advance your understanding of the social difference in the everyday, especially in sport and physical activity.

One way to think about the power of social conditions in daily interactions is to acknowledge our role in creating the meanings assigned to natural differences. That is, as citizens in the social world, we learn very early how to locate ourselves and others within falsely strict categories of difference. Sociologists call this social construction. To suggest that difference is socially constructed is not to say that difference does not exist or is not real; rather, it simply names our role in the process of defining the ways that difference should matter. Social construction is a process of defining a social phenomenon or artifact in ways that reflect values of a particular social group (e.g., nation, community, family, club, or team) in a particular moment. Therefore the meaning of youth sport in the United States is socially constructed—it reflects our capitalist-inspired beliefs, and we imagine that it helps to produce good, productive citizens. Other societies may see youth sport in very different ways and assign very different meanings and outcome expectations to youth sport. This is also a social construction because it reflects the values of a particular social group in a particular moment.

Sociologists of sport and physical activity have largely focused on race, social class, and gender in sporting spaces. Some have examined these categories of difference in exercise and physical education settings and others have ventured beyond these three categories to examine these spaces as informed and organized around sexuality and ability. To echo the introduction, researchers often focus their analyses on questions of representation or on issues of cultural beliefs, or what some sociologists refer to as **ideology**. A common and somewhat simplified definition of ideology is a set of ideas that explain the way things are currently organized and make them seem natural or real. In the following sections, we offer examples of research focused on structure and representation as well as that focused on ideologies of race, social class, gender, sexuality, and ability.

Race in Sporting, Exercising, and Schooling Spaces

Race is socially constructed meaning about physical differences, typically based on ideas about skin color, facial features, hairstyle, and body size and shape. **Racism** is systematic and institutionalized prejudice based on ideologies about race. **Racial formation** refers to a sociohistorical process by which racial categories are created, inhabited, transformed, and destroyed. According to Omi and Winant (1994), there are two steps in this process:

1. Historically situated projects (e.g., European expansionism)
2. Link with **hegemony** (e.g., ideology and structure)

Related to these two steps in the racialization process is the concept of **indigenous peoples**. Although a contested term, *indigenous* refers to groups of people who are believed to be the original inhabitants of a geographic region (e.g., the Maori in New Zealand, Dene in Canada).

Some of the most comprehensive and informative research on racial representation in sport currently comes from The Institute for Diversity and Ethics in Sport (TIDES) at the University of Central Florida. Under the direction of Dr. Richard Lapchick, whom you read about in chapter 1, TIDES compiles annual reports on racial representation in professional and collegiate sport. In many professional sports in the United States, the reports reveal a slightly variant but common pattern of high rates of representation as athletes among non-White populations (largely African American and Latino men) and high rates of representation as managers and owners by White men. The TIDES reports on professional and collegiate sport indicate racial and gender inequality in athlete rates of representation and in the rates of representation in the coaching and athletics director ranks.

While the landscape research offered through TIDES is quite informative, other important research on race in sport and physical activity doesn't count people at all. Rather, cultural research on race offers an account of the role of race in sport and the role of sport in racial ideology. Cultural research at times also accounts for the experiences of sporting, exercising, and schooling spaces as racialized spaces, or social spaces that have been organized around the dominant beliefs (ideologies) of race. That is, cultural analyses of race in sport do not assume that the mere presence of people from different racial groups indicates equity or multicultural harmony. Instead, these culture-focused scholars ask how,

governance—Formal organizational structure, policy, and rules in particular physical activity settings, especially competitive settings.

control—For social scientists, forms of institutional power to define and maintain current social structures, including sport and physical activity.

ideology—A set of ideas used to explain the way things are.

race—Socially constructed meaning about physical differences, typically based on ideas about skin color, facial features, hairstyle, and body size and shape.

racism—Systematic and institutionalized prejudice based on ideologies about race.

racial formation—A sociohistorical process by which racial categories are created, inhabited, transformed, and destroyed.

hegemony—The dominant ideology.

indigenous peoples—Groups of people who are believed to be the original inhabitants of a geographic region.

where, and when racial differences are visible in sport. For example, Doug Foley (1999) studied U.S. high school football in Texas, paying close attention to cultural divides among male students in the school setting. He found that different forms of masculinities were racialized and to some extent defined through one's relation to the high school football team. Mexican male students who were not on the football team were most often categorized as "vatos" (Mexican-identified young men), and being present at football games while not being involved in the game or concerned about the outcome of the game was crucial to their social category location. Yet Mexican male students who were on the football team were normalized toward a White middle-class framing of masculinity. Foley (1999) found that both being on the team and intentionally not being on the team culturally situated high school boys in racialized ways.

Both racial representation and cultural beliefs (ideologies) matter for a sociological perspective. Representation may indicate historic and ongoing differential access to certain sports by certain racial groups. Cultural analyses may reveal how practices remain influenced by dominant beliefs about how one ought to experience sport. It is one thing to understand the importance of Venus and Serena Williams gaining access to the very White sport of professional tennis. It is something different to understand their individual and patterned daily experiences of navigating that White (or whitened) sporting space (Douglas, 2002).

Social Class in Sporting, Exercising, and Schooling Spaces

All societies are stratified. In the United States, it is our preference to believe that our society is open and full of equal opportunity for all citizens. Sport and physical activity become social spaces where these values are promoted and also unveiled as false consciousness. **Social class** specifically refers to categories of people who share similar social positions based on economic resources like income, wealth (savings and assets), occupation, education, and social connections (Coakley, 2009). To be clear, social class is not merely about the money in your pocket but is deeply tied to the ways you earn and spend that money. It is also a cultural experience, not merely an economic accounting phenomenon. Think about your neighborhood. You probably shared some things in common with your friends. Parents in your neighborhood probably held similar types of jobs, owned the same number of cars, had similar-sized homes, and had similar amounts of time for leisure pursuits. The number of people living in each house and the level of education among adults were also likely similar in your neighborhood. This is social class coming to life and showing itself as much more than money in one's bank account.

social class—Categories of people who share similar social position based on economic resources like income, wealth (savings and assets), occupation, education, and social connections.

For example, Oprah Winfrey is a capitalist not merely because of the amount of money she has but rather because of how her economic resources situate her in a position of ownership, not just ownership of things but ownership over the production of things. Oprah didn't just own a television show; she owns the means of producing television shows (OWN channel), communication networks (magazine), and global human engagement spaces (21-day meditation).

LOOKING AT SOCIAL CLASS

Complete the chart. For each activity or item, identify three levels of costs. Certainly, upper-class people may choose to save their money and purchase the less expensive product; this chart acknowledges the various options (and lack of options) people face in purchasing and paying for sport and exercise opportunities. Some examples of basketball shoes have been filled in to get you started.

Activity	Lower income	Middle income	Upper income
Basketball shoes	Starbury One by Stephon Marbury, $13.85	Boys Nike LeBron XIII shoe, $59.99	Air Jordan 4 Retro, $190.00
Youth sport team			
Fitness club			
NBA game tickets			
NCAA football game tickets			
Additional sporting event			
Item/activity 1: your choice			
Item/activity 2: your choice			
Item/activity 3: your choice			

What conclusions can you make about the ways social class influences one's access to participation in sport and physical activity?

Quick Fact

The average ticket cost for major league baseball in 2014 was $28 per seat. The lowest ticket price for the 2014 World Series between the San Francisco Giants and the Kansas City Royals was $300 for standing room only (for the games hosted in San Francisco). The Giants, like many professional sport teams, use dynamic ticket pricing, which allows them to charge more for tickets to games against better or more popular opponents. So, a game against the Colorado Rockies may cost a fan $40, and those same seats against the rival Los Angeles Dodgers could exceed $100. The average NBA and NHL tickets in 2014 were $54 and $62, respectively. The average ticket price for the NFL was $85, the high for American average ticket prices in professional sport. Despite the contributions of taxpayers to the cost of stadiums and civic support for these professional sport teams and events, all too often, "your Yankees" and "your Dodgers" offer performances that are out of reach of most working-class members of society.

Similarly, former NBA star Magic Johnson is a capitalist who puts his power of ownership to use in typically underresourced communities.

Sociologists generally study a range of social classes, with a majority of research focused on the underclass and the middle class, in part because these groups of citizens are more likely to be significantly economically affected by societal changes but also because of their numeric majority in society. Social scientists spend more time focused on social inequalities than on the specific ways that privileged classes use their economic power to maintain it and to shape a social world that ensures the persistence of that privilege.

Gender in Sporting, Exercising, and Schooling Spaces

The role of sport and physical activity in support of dominant gender ideologies may be tied to major societal shifts like the Industrial Revolution. The shift from rural, self-sufficient living to urban, industrial living meant that men worked outside of the home, typically in factory jobs, and women remained home with the children, including male children. Looking back on this time of social and cultural change in the United States and globally, social scientists suggest that a cult of manliness developed in response to the new feminization of the home and school life of young men. Accordingly, sport and physical activity met two needs: recreation and development of proper manly behavior. Thus, if sport developed manly traits, then sport was not for girls. Given these conditions, one might imagine that sports were naturally more suited to boys than girls, but a sociological perspective tells us that our current gendered beliefs about sport and physical activity are much less natural and far more ideologically constituted through responses to structural issues over time.

Our understanding of the concept of gender has changed over time as well. To understand gender in sport and physical activity, we must distinguish between biological sex categories, or those either/or categories typically assigned at birth, and cultural constructions of gender, or the dominant beliefs about what constitutes proper male and female social behavior. Research by Nick Trujillo indicates that hegemonic masculinity is "not a unitary form of male domination [but rather] a form of male domination open to potential contradiction, ironies, and paradoxes" (1995, p. 405). Relatedly, **patriarchy** is a system of stratification based on naturalization of male dominance in all spheres of social life. It influences personal, social, and economic relations and privileges a particular form of masculinity in all forms of human interaction.

> **patriarchy**—A system of stratification based on naturalization of male dominance in all spheres of social life.

The role of sport in socializing young men and women into appropriately gendered adults has been a common topic for sociologists of sport and physical activity. Yet research focused on more than representation or rates of participation often indicates that gender is not as simple a category as one would assume. In fact, elite sport especially creates social conditions and arrangements where members of society may act in contradictory ways to gain the most social and physical benefit from the activity. For example, women in bodybuilding often contend with mixed messages

 ## WOMEN'S SPORTS FOUNDATION

The Women's Sports Foundation (WSF) was established in 1974 by tennis player and women's sports advocate Billie Jean King. The WSF offers sport and physical activity programming for girls across the United States. It also provides funding for female athletes in Olympic and Paralympic sports. The WSF also publishes reports related to participation in girls' sports, Title IX, homophobia, and gender equity in the Olympic and Paralympic Games. More recently, the WSF partnered with the University of Michigan to create the SHARP Center (Sport, Health, and Activity Research and Policy Center for Women and Girls). The SHARP Center is working to establish itself as a world-class research center on topics related to girls and women in sports.

© AP Photo

Women's Sports Foundation founder Billie Jean King playing tennis.

gender—How one is identified as male or female; while sex may be the biological term related to one's genitalia, gender is socially constructed and refers to the ways we think about masculinity and femininity.

sexuality—A person's preference as related to sexual desires, including asexual, bisexual, heterosexual, and homosexual.

sexual orientation—A person's attraction in terms of sexual partners.

about building muscle and maintaining a feminine form. There are no natural reasons that big muscles are equated with masculinity, yet in this competitive sporting space, male and female muscled bodies get judged differently. These judgments are informed by cultural preferences for an obvious two-category gender system.

In another example, R.W. Connell (1990) illustrated contradictions in the role of elite sport performance and preferred masculine identity. Connell observed the training of an Ironman competitor. The Ironman is a long-distance triathlon involving a 26-mile run, 112-mile (180 km) bike ride, and 2.4-mile (3.9 km) ocean swim. The number of people who have completed this event at an elite level remains small. Therefore, one would expect all sorts of beneficial social status would be bestowed on and enjoyed by such a man. Contrary to popular belief, this Ironman was too tired and too restricted by his training to also enjoy the perceived social benefits of such an identity. While on a surface level, the Ironman enjoyed a secure, preferred masculine identity, he simultaneously lived a sporting life that restricted his ability to enjoy that virile manliness. These research examples suggest that sport can be a space where gender is unveiled as a more complex social category of difference. At the same time, the basic structure of the sporting space may solidify a two-category gender system through its reductionist rules.

Sexuality in Sporting, Exercising, and Schooling Spaces

For sociologists, sexuality is a crucial social category and organizing principle in our daily lives. Related to each of the other social categories and often treated as identical to **gender**, sexuality is actually a powerful category of social difference in itself. **Sexuality** refers to choices in sex practices, family structures, and physical and emotional desires. As stated previously, social class is difficult to talk about honestly because we do not like to believe that the United States could operate on an unequal social system. Similarly, sexuality is challenging to discuss in any public manner because American cultural values tell us that sexuality and sex acts

 Quick Fact

Have you ever thought about how much it costs to participate in triathlons? *The Globe and Mail* (Canada) tallied up the costs, in addition to the time commitment to prepare for the event (McAlaster, 2013). The entry fee for Ironman Canada in 2013 was $702 ($675 with a $27 service fee; prices in Canadian dollars). They provided a list of additional costs, such as a pool membership, bicycle maintenance, and nutrition. Conclusion? It costs a lot of money to participate in Ironman events! Similarly, the entry fee for the New York City marathon, which attracts more than 50,000 entrants (from a lottery system), is more than $250 for the 26.2-mile course.

MAGAZINES AS MESSENGERS

Content analysis is another method of data collection. Observing the dominant ideas that are present in magazines can be deeply revealing about society and culture. For this activity, select a magazine that addresses sport, exercise, or physical activity. Using the magazine as your data source, complete the chart.

Primary categories	Social groups	Number of photos	Number of articles
Gender	Female		
	Male		
Race and ethnicity	African American		
	Asian/Pacific Islander		
	Caucasian		
	Hispanic/Latino		
	Biracial or multiracial		
Age	Youth		
	Young adult		
	Adult		
	Older adult		
Physical status	Able bodied		
	Person with disability		

Review your results.

1. What patterns exist in your magazine?

2. What messages does the magazine transmit in their inclusion and exclusion of certain groups?

3. What factors would influence a magazine about including or excluding a certain group?

4. How might the messages vary by media form (such as radio, television, Internet)?

are private matters. In actuality, sexuality as a social organizing principle is all over our public lives—expectations for a dominant or preferred moral expression of sexuality, **sexual orientation**, and marriage partners are part and parcel of mundane interactions. Recall that social science invites one to observe moral stances as neither right nor wrong but reflective of the most dominant preferred forms of acting. For example, until very recently when same-sex marriage rights became U.S. law, when your friend's two moms who were not allowed to be legally married went to the gym to buy a family membership, they might not have qualified for the family category, which would have required them to pay more for their membership than a heterosexual couple would pay. Additionally, your transgender teammate may find everyday public facilities like restrooms to be socially risky spaces, and gendered

Quick Fact

There is not a database of gay athletes. Instead, we're left with anecdotal evidence and personal stories and experiences. No link exists between playing sport and sexual orientation. Although the public perception is that most female athletes are lesbians, there are no data to support such beliefs. Nor are there data to support the belief that a sport like football makes boys into men (i.e., heterosexual men).

school policies may curtail their place on the team, especially in the absence of trans allies and trans-friendly policies. The fact that these two categories of people fall outside of standard membership and public facility policy reveals the ways that seemingly innocent personal values actually flow into daily physical activity structures and create what are called structural inequalities.

Sociologists of sport and physical activity observe sporting, exercising, and schooling spaces as already sexualized spaces—cultural spaces, sport teams, gyms, and schools reflect dominant beliefs about sexuality. For example, in sport, it is expected that elite male athletes in most sports are heterosexual and indeed that the sport experience develops one's "natural" heterosexuality. In women's elite sport, it is a commonly held belief that dedicated elite sport involvement leads to lesbianism. In fact, some women have suggested that their sport choices centered on not being labeled a lesbian. This sort of assertion of one's sexuality can be present for young men in sport as well. Dr. Michael Messner (2000) conducted an autoethnographic study, or a study in which he reexamined his own sport experience through a sociological lens. Using a methodology of memory work, Dr. Messner recounted a vivid experience of a basketball game in which he intentionally harmed another boy on the court. His sociologically informed recollection suggests that this overexertion of physical power during the game was not random; in fact, it was crucial in establishing his own heterosexuality. As Messner tells the story, each of the boys on the court already had social identities and statuses related to their school and community settings, and this young man was on the edge, close to not performing the preferred heterosexual masculinity of their cultural space—therefore, he became a productive target of Messner's sport-related aggression.

As we apply our sociological perspective, we can imagine such a scene, where the simplest of actions—like knocking someone to the ground while fielding a rebound—are always already deeply tied to larger societal issues. None of the boys present had to talk about sexuality, yet in that moment, the sporting actions embodied an antigay, proheterosexual, dominantly masculine identity for all present. In more current times, one may relate this story to that of the NFL hazing incidents between athletes Richie Incognito and Jonathan Martin (Glauber, 2013). One is hesitant to believe that an NFL athlete could be physically or mentally intimidated by another human being, but this was indeed the case on the Miami Dolphins squad in 2013. Unlike the preceding Messner example, this case became about a racialized masculinity that was expected of both the hazer and the athlete being hazed. Again, sport served as a space for socializing people toward preferred social roles and subjectivities.

⭐ HUDSON TAYLOR, ATHLETE ALLY

Hudson Taylor is a wrestling coach at Columbia University and the founder of Athlete Ally, an organization that educates, encourages, and empowers straight athletes to fight homophobia and transphobia in sport. Many professional athletes representing a variety of sports have joined Athlete Ally. Athlete Ally offers programming for school-aged children and college students. Recently, the organization worked to draw attention to the antigay legislation and practices of Russia, the host nation of the 2014 Sochi Winter Olympic and Paralympic Games. Athlete Ally also collected signatures to urge the IOC to uphold Principle 6, the part of the Olympic Charter proclaiming sport as a human right for all.

Disability in Sporting, Exercising, and Schooling Spaces

Physicality refers to the socially constructed categories of physical bodies, often related to mobility issues. A medical model applied to disability and sport suggests that physically or mentally impaired bodies are deficient individual bodies that need to be fixed in order to gain access to mainstream sport. A social minority model suggests the deficiency is in the social conditions that constrain people, not in the people themselves. Thus, the focus is on eliminating all kinds of disabling conditions in society (Freund, 2001). In fact, Coakley (2009) suggested that an impairment becomes a disability only when social conditions are not or cannot be made to allow that person full participation. For sociologists of sport and physical activity, it is most productive to examine and consider the numerous ways that sport, exercise, and schooling spaces create disabling conditions for members of society who might otherwise choose to be physically active.

Disability is perhaps the most segregated topic among those of difference and diversity in sport. By segregated, we mean to suggest that even though many social scientists aim to analyze the intersecting nature of various social categories of difference (e.g., race, class, gender), the category of disability tends to be either ignored or analyzed in isolation. This is not entirely accurate. For example, Emma Stone (2001) examined Chinese nationalism and the symbolic power of visible war heroes whose public presence in major disability sporting events may create an idea that the Chinese nation takes care of all of its people, regardless of their physical ability. As well, some social scientists are asking questions about the societal infrastructure or program, facility, and funds resources for sport and physical activity involvement of people with physical or mental impairments in developing countries (Lauff, 2011). This is important research, since the United Nations and World Health Organization indicate that 80 percent of the world's disabled live in developing countries (United Nations Enable, n.d.).

Given the number of people affected by an impairment, this pattern of isolated study of disability and physical activity is odd and limiting for our overall understanding of sport in the lives of diversely situated people. For example, DePauw and Gavron (2005) reported that people living, working, and playing with physical or mental impairments have been part of society forever. In fact, it is estimated that

15 percent of the world's population live with some form of disability, and people whose life expectancy is 70 years of age will typically spend about 8 years living with a disability (United Nations Enable, n.d.). In the current historical moment, rates of living with various impairments are increasing as the result of population growth, medical advances, and the aging process. These trends will need to be addressed by kinesiologists and all who care about physical activity as part of an overall quality of life. DePauw and Gavron brought sport into the broader conversation about disability and social justice and offered insights to the changing social landscape for disability sport and physical education. Their work indicates that 20th-century legislation, media coverage, and technical advances have contributed to a more visible presence of people living with impairments in society. As you may have noticed during the 2012 London Olympic Games, there was also a clear partnership between the "able-bodied" Games and the Paralympic Games that followed in the same venue. The London Paralympic Games were the most-watched Paralympic Games in recorded history, after years of being neglected in the news media, and the elite performances of athletes whose times and scores are, in some sports, just seconds off of those of their able-bodied cohort may have garnered a newly dedicated audience.

Despite the gains seen in media coverage and fandom in recent years, research by Toni Bruce indicates that the mainstream media tends to celebrate disabled athletes who are most "like us," or those whose impairments do not make them hard to watch or to cheer on (2014). Moreover, Purdue and Howe (2013) studied the hierarchies that exist within sport governing bodies such as the International Paralympic Committee (IPC), especially because the IPC decides which disabled athletes are allowed to compete. In both the media coverage and the governance of disability sport, the authors also draw attention to a shared desire to create a consistent consumer for these profit-motivated sport businesses—remember that elite competitive sport is often focused on profit. Often, the least differently abled athletes and the most functional, most aesthetically pleasing disabled athletes are the ones the media selects to represent all disabled athletes and the ones the IPC selects to compete in these hypermediated sporting competitions. Some disability scholars refer to these preferred disabled athletes as "the superhumans" and might suggest

 PARALYMPICS IN PRIME TIME

At the 2014 Sochi Paralympics and the 2106 Rio Paralympics, American television network NBC committed to an unprecedented 116 hours of coverage. In previous coverage, Paralympic sport was shown to the audience post-Paralympics in a 1- to 2-hour show of highlights.

1. What might account for the increase in coverage of Paralympic athletes?

2. How do you suspect NBC will attract viewers to these events?

that even as access and media coverage increase, there remains a strong preference for profit over social justice in the role of elite disability sport.

Other scholars have posed questions about the very idea of disability and projects of inclusion in the U.S. educational system (Promis, Erevelles, & Matthews, 2001). Still others have conducted in-depth narrative research regarding impairment sustained through sport involvement, whether it be an acute event or long-term wear and tear on the body (Smith, 2013). Such research may offer insight to best practices in school-based physical activity programs and increasingly seeks experiential knowledge from the very students and athletes living with impairments. Beyond elite sport, research that focuses on everyday physical activity such as crossing a busy street, lifting groceries, or simply enjoying a walk in the outdoors, Peter Freund (2001) suggested that we focus on addressing "disabling conditions" rather than identifying individual people as disabled. For Freund, it is clear that there are many differently abled bodies living in our everyday worlds, and it is our collective responsibility to imagine public spaces and even sporting spaces that are accessible to all people. Any kinesiologist with a social science skill set ought to be able to consider cognitive and physical impairments as they design and implement physical activity programs that do not create disabling conditions.

Intersecting Inequalities

Thus far, we have treated social categories as though they each act independently of the others, but if you are truly applying your emergent sociological imagination, you may have already noticed that these categories overlap considerably. Sociologists of sport and physical activity refer to this overlap of social categories as intersections, cross-cutting social organizing principles, and sometimes even "prisms of difference" (Baca Zinn, Hondagneu-Sotelo, & Messner, 2010). The point of intersectional analyses is to demonstrate how these categories of difference work together to organize our social lives and to illuminate how we each navigate and negotiate these categories of difference in our everyday lives.

One way that sociologists of sport and physical activity describe this dominant intersectional inequality in our daily lives is through a framework that identifies the ways that one's location in a privileged racial, social, or economic category is constantly shaping how one experiences other forms of difference. Thinking back to the Foley (1999) research on high school football, Mexican high school students experienced an intersecting set of privilege or disadvantage based on their gender, sport affiliation, social class, and racial or ethnic status. Despite our deep desire to see sport and physical activity as social spaces that are free from prejudice, they are not. In fact, the three components of access, atmosphere, governance, and control illuminate a cross-cutting power assigned to difference that situates participants in different relations to the potential benefits of physical activity participation. Chapter 6 explores how difference is both exploited and controlled by nations in order to produce a national story of multicultural harmony and global superiority.

The Short of It

- All societies are stratified, meaning that the makeup of people in any societal space reflects a historical legacy of human movement, sharing of ideas, merging of languages, and of course different access to power in determining how social difference matters.

- Sociologists of sport and physical activity have focused their analytic attention on issues of *access*, *atmosphere*, *governance*, and *control*.

- In sociology of sport and physical activity, the primary categories of social difference under analysis have been race, social class, gender, sexuality, and ability.

- Social difference is natural and ever present, and the social hierarchies attached to this social difference are created by people. They are socially constructed rather than based in any sort of evidence.

CHAPTER

Sport and Physical Activity in National and International Unity

In this chapter you will learn the following:

✓ How sociologists define and study the nation, nationalism, and nation building
✓ The relationships between sport, physical activity, and nationalism
✓ How sport, globalization, and citizenship are interrelated
✓ The role of sport and the mass media in national identity projects

> Sport has the power to change the world.
>
> **Nelson Mandela**

Do you remember cheering for your favorite team or athlete during the Olympic Games? Do you have relatives or friends from outside your country who took great pride when their home country did well in the Olympics or other international sporting event? When someone mentions the nations of the United States, Canada, Brazil, or Romania, which sports come to mind? You have probably learned to associate baseball, hockey, soccer, and gymnastics with these countries, respectively. And what ideas do you hold about countries that boycott the Olympic Games or that do not allow women to compete on their teams? Each of these questions offers you a chance to aim your sociological imagination at sport and physical activity in national and global contexts.

The relevance of sporting traditions to national identities and the use of sport in support of nationalist propaganda are of keen interest to sociologically informed kinesiologists. In fact, some might say that the sociology of sport began as a field motivated to understand and articulate the importance of sport to a nation's development, especially in creating a consensus association among a nation's citizens. Consider the Olympic Games and the pride certain countries have in dominating particular sports or in competing among the top nations in the medal count. Remember your own childhood and which sports were most relevant in your school, community, and leisure experiences—perhaps involvement in these activities created a sense of belonging, purpose, and unity?

While much of the current research on physical culture and **nationalism** focuses on sport, the field of study we know today as kinesiology emerged in part out of concerns for the health and wellness of the nation. At times this concern for the nation was centered on the effects of major societal change like that of a shift from farm living to city living brought about by industrialization. In other times, the concern for the nation was more directly about national security and a perceived ability to protect one's nation should it encounter conflict with other nations. In times of war, such concerns may have informed a national curriculum for K-12 physical education. In other times, concerns may have informed educational planning without developing a firm national curriculum. In any case, despite a more current focus on sport in relation to the nation, other physical activity settings, including physical education and leisure, have also been deeply linked to nation building.

This chapter describes the relationship between sport and physical activity in national and global perspectives. Let's start by considering two guiding perspectives in the sociological study of sport and physical activity: sport *of* the nation and sport *for* the nation. **Sport of the nation** illuminates the ways that sport emerges in all nations as a reflection of the historical, political, and cultural conditions of a particular nation. For example, in the United States, several political, historical, and cultural conditions ensured that baseball became our national pastime rather than, for example, lacrosse, a sport that can be located with original inhabitants of U.S. lands. Those same conditions contributed to football's overtaking baseball as the nation's pastime. Alternatively, a focus on **sport for the nation** identifies the ways that sporting practices may be used to disseminate dominant national beliefs and ideals; sporting events offer a national and global stage for asserting those nationalist beliefs and agendas. Currently, sociologically informed kinesiologists are also interested in global relations and the use of sport for development projects. If you recall previous discussions about functional and conflict theorizing in sociology, you will realize that both of these perspectives are useful, especially since they invite very different analytic frames for the link between sport and nation. The application of these perspectives allows social scientists and emergent cultural observers to analyze how sport and physical activity may act to unify or divide nations and may ameliorate or exacerbate contentious geopolitical issues.

nationalism—Political set of beliefs or ideologies related to how people come to connect with their country and sense of national identity.

sport of the nation—Illuminates the ways that sport emerges in all nations as a reflection of the historical, political, and cultural conditions of a particular nation.

sport for the nation—Identifies the ways that sporting practices may be used to disseminate dominant national beliefs and ideals; sporting events offer a national and global stage for asserting those nationalist beliefs and agendas.

nation—Typically considered a society that occupies a particular territory but also reflects dominant ideas about the nation influenced by global histories, economics, and politics.

Linking Sport to the Nation

Generally, a **nation** is considered to be a society that occupies a particular territory, but we must consider historical context and global economic goals as major influences in our imagination of the nation. Some scholars suggest that it is in war and sport that the nation most obviously comes to matter as citizens fight and ration for their nation and fans support and cheer for their side in each activity, respectively. For example, a visit to the museum at Wimbledon will reveal a history of the tennis

Quick Fact

Did you know that during WWII, the Wimbledon Championships were cancelled, a portion of the All England Club land was repurposed as farmland to support the troops, and German bombs actually landed at center court on October 11, 1940? Even today, there remains a visible, although voluntary, corps of the United Kingdom Armed Forces at the Wimbledon Championships Tournament (Klein, 2012). Examples such as this suggest significant links between sport and nations and invite a careful consideration of the establishment of nations or the nation-state.

grounds' becoming a crucial agricultural resource during WWII, especially because other farmlands had been ravaged by war (Klein, 2012).

Social scientists have long relied on the nation as the object of scientific analysis. That is, the sense making of how societies operate and what constitutes their working parts has historically been informed by observations of nation-states, or sovereign geopolitical spaces that operate as self-governed entities in the broader social world. Most social scientists attribute the concept of the modern nation-state to the Bretton Woods Conference in 1944, where 44 delegate nations, including the post–World War II major world powers of France, Britain, Germany, Japan, and the United States, decided for the world that the "sovereign nation" (a self-governing, self-sufficient nation) was the most desirable organizing and stabilizing unit for a global humanity. What is often left out of descriptions of this benevolent move is the fact that these imperialist nations found it too costly to rule over so many other countries; therefore, the new virtue of sovereignty seemed a fine consensus. Thus, after decades of imperial rule and colonial relations, these superpowers found a new way to protect their ruling profit from those they ruled and to appear benevolent in that process.

The idea of nation-states was not completely absent of good will—several supranational structures were initiated to assist all nations in finding their place in a new global order. The World Bank, International Monetary Fund, and United Nations were formed around this time to stabilize a global economy, offer support to new nation-states with transitioning economies, and provide security and peacekeeping forces in and among new nation-states where new borders and citizenship policies may cause factional fighting. Social sciences tell us, however, that even these well-intentioned supranational structures became part of a set of global conditions that created new inequalities and hierarchies among nations rather than simply stabilizing a global governance and economic system. In effect, all sovereign states wishing to be recognized by and receive support from these supranational entities had to vow to develop into a similar, capitalist-friendly nation. As you might imagine, this one-size-fits-all model of nationhood did not actually fit all nations. As nations continued to evolve in various hierarchical contexts of development, sport (more so than physical activity) became a highly visible representation of the health and wealth of a nation.

In fact, Bairner suggested that "sport will play a part in allowing nations to resist global homogenization, [while] at the same time, however, it will also continue to reflect the fact that national identity is a contentious and contested issue, even in stable western democracies" (2001, p. 177). For example, according to Bairner, sport becomes a crucial social space for parsing out contested national identity politics such as those between Francophone and Anglophone Canadians, or "old" and "new" Swedes, or English cricketers of Pakistani origin. To explain this significant role of sport in national identity development, Bairner suggested three specific connections:

- Sporting nationalism is closely linked with political nationalism.
- Neither sporting nor political nationalism is ever as homogenous or superficial as readings might suggest.
- By examining the links between sport and the formation of specific national identities, we may unveil the complex character of nationality.

PETER DONNELLY, CENTRE FOR SPORT POLICY STUDIES

Peter Donnelly is a professor at the University of Toronto. He earned his PhD at the University of Massachusetts at Amherst. His scholarship on a range of topics has greatly influenced the field of sport sociology. His research interests lie in sport subcultures, including rock climbers and adventure sport participants, children in sport, and sport policy. To that end, Donnelly and his colleague at the University of Toronto, Bruce Kidd, established the Centre for Sport Policy Studies in 1999. Among the goals of the centre are making sport accessible and equitable for all and establishing an educational mandate for sport in educational institutions. The centre hosts conferences and seminars and has ongoing projects that result in reports and other publications that directly reflect and inform national and supranational conditions for sport in Canada.

Photo courtesy of Peter Donnelly.

Sport and Nationalism

Some sociologists of sport, such as Alan Bairner, study the role of sport in the development of nationalism, or the social process of **collective identity formation**. This collective identity formation brings people's own identification with their nation into alignment with the nation's political contours. So, through sport, one learns to identify with the nation; by identifying with the nation's preferred set of values and goals, one supports the rules of the nation. For example, if you wish to join the baseball team because its members are excellent at baseball and schoolwork, then part of your pride in membership will be linked to how well you also may represent these two forms of excellence. In this way, you identify with the idea of the team's goals and values. Then by your actions you actually enforce the team's goals and values—you study as often as you work on your fastball. The same is true of one's national identity formation. Bairner suggested that national identities are rooted in both human imagination and materiality (reality) and that myth making and the invention of tradition are two key elements. Sport is a crucial aspect of this myth making and invention of tradition.

For example, in American nation building, sport played a role in various key material and symbolic moments. Early in the nation's establishment, American team sport became a social space where people could perform an allegiance to their new host country rather than maintain ties to the sporting games and rituals of a prior home (e.g., cricket and rugby from Britain). Similarly, the growth and stabilization of particular team sports (e.g., baseball, football, and basketball) became markers of particular American culture. Clubs, school curricula, and leisure activities extended this new culture to the process of

collective identity formation— The process one goes through to feel a shared sense of belonging to a group.

community building, or national identity formation. Along the way, this establishment of particular American team sports as central to national identity served also to separate Americans from their former British colonizers and to marginalize the rituals and games of Native American communities. For those of us who have lived much of our lives in the United States, the American-ness of baseball, football, and basketball may seem natural and even original to our country, but these are examples of inventing traditions and preferred histories. If you are applying your sociological imagination, you may ask the following questions at this point: Why didn't lacrosse

 # PING-PONG DIPLOMACY, 1972

In April 1971, the American table tennis team was invited to compete against the Chinese table tennis team in what has become known as Ping-Pong diplomacy. Although U.S. President Richard Nixon longed to visit China (some say he wanted their assistance in the Vietnam War), Americans had not visited China since 1949, and the two countries suffered a strained relationship. When the U.S. table tennis team competed in China, it symbolically opened the door for Nixon to visit China the following year. In this sense, sport served as the opening act of a dance between the two countries as they sought to improve their relationship. In China, this historic event is taught to all Chinese students in their middle school years, though in the United States, many adults are still unfamiliar with the international sporting event that altered the relationship between the two nations. Table tennis is played by more than 300 million Chinese citizens, and the country dominates world competition in the sport. Though table tennis is marginalized in the United States, the sport is a source of national pride for China.

John Rooney/AP/Press Association Images

Citizens of the United States would probably be surprised to hear that a table tennis tournament holds such political and historical weight, but at one time it helped to reopen the political door between the United States and China.

Quick Fact

The International Olympic Committee's views on nationalism are quite complicated. In fact, the sporting body has rules about who can compete for which country. At the 2010 Winter Games in Vancouver, American Allison Reed competed for the Republic of Georgia in figure skating, though Reed had never even visited the country. Allison's siblings competed for Japan at the Vancouver Games, based on their mother's Japanese citizenship. The IOC has rules related to eligibility, making it possible for an athlete to compete for one country in one Olympic Games and a different country in a subsequent Olympic Games, revealing the ways citizenship and nationality can be fluid rather than fixed.

become a national sport in the United States? If soccer has been played in the United States for so long, why has it not caught on as an American sport like the others? These are good questions that reflect Bairner's contention that nationalism is complicated and constantly linked with current political affairs.

To be clear, for sport sociologists, *nation* is a contested term. Some scholars focus on geographic and political representations of the nation, while others, like Bairner, argue that the nation exists simultaneously in a material, geographic, and political realm and in an imaginary manner (or a manner characterized by one's ideas about the nation and belonging). As Benedict Anderson (1983) articulated, we live in imagined communities, existing as nations in both limited and sovereign contexts. That is, we come to imagine ourselves as members of such nations even though we will likely never meet most of the other members. We understand the nation as having borders that limit the span of the nation while also imagining the nation as offering equal membership among all citizens. Anderson's ideas suggest that we feel American or Iranian or Korean (or any other national belonging) both because of residing in that respective nation and because of our imagining of what that nation represents through its preferred languages, ideas, and citizens.

Toward this end, Bairner articulated several types of nationalism, including **ethnic nationalism**, which he explained as an exclusive form of membership based on natural origins of the nation and tied to cultural links such as language and racial or ethnic belonging. Based on approved membership, **civic nationalism** is considered inclusive, since people may voluntarily join and leave the nation, as long as they are willing to follow the rules of citizenship. Finally, **sporting nationalism** represents personal connections to one's nation through sporting teams or sports in general. Given these varied forms of nationalism, a sociologically informed kinesiology professional may consider both the role of sport in the development of national identities and the development of sporting nationalisms as a response to emergent global forces.

ethnic nationalism—An exclusive form of membership based on natural origins of the nation and tied to cultural links such as language and racial or ethnic belonging.

civic nationalism—An inclusive form of membership in which people can decide their level of participation and belonging and of identifying as a citizen of a nation.

sporting nationalism—Personal connections to one's nation through sporting teams, most often national sport teams representing the nation at international sporting events such as the World Cup and the Olympics.

Sport as Unifying

When sport unifies people, it typically does so through global sporting events that invite patriotism, or a deep association with one's home nation and feeling of harmonious collectivity. Much of the social science research around sport as unifying focuses on mega-sporting events such as the Olympic Games, Commonwealth Games, FIFA World Cup, Ryder Cup, and Solheim Cup. These sorts of mega-sporting events create a world stage for competition among nation-states, and the sporting competitions create social spaces for feelings of national belonging and collectivity. More regional sporting events may also be unifying, such as the Cricket Championships, which reflect a history of colonialism, and more recently have offered sovereign nations a chance to compete against their former ruling nations, possibly creating feelings of unification and collective progress toward the nation's liberation (Rumford, 2007).

In addition to opportunities to cheer for one's nation, pivotal historic moments also provide a context for sport to play a unifying role in a nation. In the United States, following the attacks on September 11, 2001 (9/11), sport became a space for uniting and healing. Yankee Stadium was used for a multidenominational ceremony to mark the tragedy and remember those who died or suffered due to the events of 9/11. In this moment, the heroes were not athletes but soldiers, first responders, and political leaders, yet athletes shared their hallowed sporting ground for this recognition. The silencing of professional sport for more than a week following the attacks was another marker of the solidarity of sports heroes with national defense heroes. The reopening of professional sport marked a perseverance of the nation and return to a normal, free American life. Consider the symbolic power of a baseball stadium, filled to capacity with fans who felt safe in their homeland to gather among their neighbors and enjoy something as simplistically American as a baseball game. In these moments, sport was not merely about the physical act but was also deeply tied to the preferred cultural values of the nation, of an imagined American way of life.

Similarly, when South Korean Olympian Sohn Kee-Chung carried the Olympic torch into the stadium in Seoul, South Korea, for the 1988 Summer Games, his very presence marked the resilience of and global reemergence of a particular South Korean nationalism. Sohn was the gold medalist at the 1936 Summer Games marathon in Berlin, Germany. At that time, a unified Korean nation was under the

 KEY NATIONALIST MOMENTS IN SPORT

- 1968 Mexico City Games (first time a developing nation hosted; symbol of human rights)
- 1980 Lake Placid Olympic Games ("Miracle on Ice" during Cold War conflict)
- 1988 Seoul Games (symbol of economic recovery)
- 2000 Sydney Games (symbol of racial harmony and national healing)

By the late 1980s, the international campaign [against apartheid sport] had effectively barred athletes from the apartheid sector of South African sport from competing virtually everywhere in the world and stopped athletes and teams from other countries from travelling to South Africa to play. . . . It was the most sustained, internationally coordinated campaign for justice in sport the world has ever seen.

Bruce Kidd (2010)

imperial rule of Japan, and Sohn was forced to compete for the Japanese nation under the name Son Kitei. So, more than 50 years later and after several battles for independence, Sohn's presence at the opening ceremonies of the 1988 Seoul Summer Games became symbolic of healing, perseverance, and strength of a previously embattled nation. The fact that South Korea had the infrastructure and financial means to host the Olympic Games was a powerful symbol of the nation's emergence as a solvent and sovereign nation. Despite this fact, nations are judged by their members. For example, the presence of elite marathoner Sohn Kee-Chung solidified the global message that South Korea had arrived in the global era.

Another example, perhaps less spectacular, is the resilience of an economically challenged community in Odessa, Texas. You might know this story through the television show and movie *Friday Night Lights*. As previously mentioned, these major entertainment productions were generated from the ethnographic social science research of H.G. Bissinger (1990) during the late 1980s. Bissinger's research demonstrated the role of high school football in holding a town together after a major economic downturn. As well, the research shows the role of high school football in creating spaces for otherwise divided communities to come together to cheer for their school. These unifications, even if momentary, happened across race and socioeconomic class and extended beyond the Friday night football games. The extension of community resources to those involved in this valued football team resembled what Bourdieu referred to as "cultural capital" and "social capital" (1986, para. 5, 19). Make no mistake, despite Bissinger's focus on one town in one state, the values, beliefs, and social structures underlying his study are representative of the nation. Perhaps the most important insight from Bissinger's research is that even particular communities, such as Odessa, rely on everyday spaces of sport (e.g., high school football) to enact and solidify the core values of the nation.

 Quick Fact

In 2015, the Department of Defense paid 14 NFL teams more than $5 million of taxpayer dollars over a period of three seasons to promote the American military at football games. Did you happen to attend a game where soldiers unfurled a field-sized flag? You may have contributed to the funding!

Quick Fact

One could learn some confusing geography (and political) lessons by watching the Olympic Games. After World War II, East Germany and West Germany competed as two separate countries in the Games. When the Berlin Wall fell, the two countries merged to form a unified German team. Similarly, the once-dominant Soviet Union disbanded to become much smaller (and less dominant) countries after the end of the USSR. China and Taiwan compete as two separate national Olympic committees, despite the fact that Taiwan is part of China. In some ways, the IOC is able to exert enough power to cajole a country to shift their politics in exchange for admission and acceptance into the Olympic Movement.

Sport as Divisive

To the extent that sport is successful in garnering patriotic support, it may also be divisive along geopolitical boundaries. The same 1936 Berlin Games that produced Sohn Kee-Chung's marathon victory were notoriously known as the Aryan Games (these games are also referred to as the Nazi Olympics), reflecting a historical moment that was meant to demonstrate the supremacy of a new socialist (fascist) Germany. One may also consider the Cold War, roughly a 50-year state of political tension and military rivalry between nations that consistently stopped short of full-scale war. This tension largely existed between the United States and Soviet Union after World War II and marked an ideological struggle between democracy and communism. The Cold War began in the 1940s and ended in 1991 with the breakup of the Soviet Union and the collapse of the Berlin Wall, signifying the reunification of Germany. In the United States, the Cold War era produced a period of unparalleled suspicion, hostility, and persecution. This included anti-Communist hysteria; sacrifice of constitutional rights; hearings against employees who were accused of being disloyal to the government; increases in bomb shelters, air raid drills in schools, and civilian anti-Communist organizations; and suspicion of anyone whose ideas, behavior, personal life, or appearance suggested belief in or sympathy for Communism. It also had a negative influence on the U.S. economy, including sharp inflation, high fuel prices, high rates of unemployment, and enormous government budget deficits.

In this context of political tension and local suspicions, sport became a crucial space in which to prove one's patriotism and the nation's superiority. The 1980 Winter Games in Lake Placid, New York, stand out as a moment when sport became crucially tied to national sentiment. Remembered largely for the "Miracle on Ice" victory over the Soviet Union, the 1980 Olympics were one in which America's sporting victories were an important piece in the Cold War between the United States and the USSR. Sports were a much safer venue than the battlefield. In more recent times, the return to sport and use of sport stadiums for community gatherings after the events of September 11, 2001, also stand out as sport nationalism. In moments such as these, sport becomes what we call representative of the nation and our imagination of the nation. Athletes and teams become representatives of the United States versus the Soviets, or the United States versus the "terrorists." Spectators identify themselves with these nationalist competitors—they come to feel they and their values are represented by these athletes and teams. Victory in these moments becomes an index of that nation's superiority and righteousness. Similarly, nationalism is a process of creating a collective identity through staging "us versus them" moments, retelling myths, delivering propaganda, participating in rituals that reflect fidelity to the nation (e.g., pledge of allegiance, national anthem, raising of flags at medal ceremonies), and taking pride in representatives of the nation.

Most of us are much more attuned to positive, unifying aspects of local and global sport events, but social scientists have also identified the divisive nature of sport. Again, let's look at Doug Foley's (1999) enduring insights about the culture of high school sport in the United States. They reveal the role of sport in constructing subcultural groups and a hierarchical order among those groups, where male athletes in team sports often occupy the top of the social hierarchy. In his ethnographic research,

 NFL AND U.S. NATIONAL SECURITY

Schimmel (2012) examined the security practices of the NFL and the U.S. Department of Homeland Security's counterterrorism agenda, and the relationship between the two entities. With security questions and issues becoming more commonplace, especially after September 11, Schimmel suggested that citizens are playing greater roles in the everyday security operations of keeping America safe, including at sporting events. Citizens as participants in these activities illustrate the concept of resilience. After September 11, the Super Bowl was designated as a National Special Security Event, which allowed for an expansion of government and NFL intrusion into fan behavior (and that of non-fans residing in the geographic location). Schimmel provided a listing and explanation for a number of partnerships between the NFL and Department of Homeland Security related to game day security, including crowd management techniques, Operation Game Day (targeting illegal immigrants attending the Super Bowl), fan code of conduct, pat-downs of fans, and the partnership between the NFL with the Pentagon security contractor GTSI to install Virtual Private Network–encrypted video cameras in the Super Bowl host stadium and city (to remain after the Super Bowl). Schimmel suggested that the adoption of the National Infrastructure Protection Plan in 2009 cemented the NFL with the U.S. national security agenda, allowing for unprecedented institutionalized relationship between NFL team owners, facility managers, and the Department of Homeland Security. Fans were then set up as citizen soldiers and asked to report suspicious behavior, which abdicated the NFL and the U.S. government from any game day security issues because of its battlefield designation.

1. Do you think most fans know of their responsibilities as "citizen soldiers"?

2. What factors do you believe would contribute to fans accepting or rejecting such responsibilities?

Foley described the depth and process of cultural difference making and the ways that core organizing principles such as race, gender, and social class collude with sport to maintain preferred social hierarchies. Like the work of Bissinger, these local social hierarchies that are constructed through high school sport reflect broader ideas about the nation, including which citizens belong at the top and ought to serve as representatives of the nation (e.g., male football athletes). Unlike our focus on the unifying aspects of Bissinger's field of study, Foley's research illuminated the potential for divisiveness within and through high school sport.

Often, events that are meant to be unifying are also divisive, especially given social hierarchies and their largely invisible daily work to maintain themselves. Even though sport may be considered to contribute to national healing, it may simultaneously create new and support old social divisions. Kyle Kusz (2007) studied the media rhetoric around NASCAR and the death of former NFL player turned soldier Pat Tillman after September 11. It is important to note the specific way that Kusz named a particular form of American nationalism. Specifically, he referred to new racial hierarchies and daily governance of bodies as a "White cultural nationalism" (p. 77). According to Kusz, in the aftermath of the violent events of September 11, 2001, where fundamentalist activists enacted a series of airplane hijackings and destroyed American government and capitalist structures, Whitened sports such as NASCAR and White athletic heroes such as Pat Tillman came to represent the nation. Kusz suggested that a post–September 11 White cultural nationalism is a dominant way of explaining current social conditions through particular "nationalist narratives, symbols, and imagery drenched in a patriotism that simultaneously revives and recirculates culturally familiar images of White men who are at once common . . . and exceptionally heroic in leading the fight to protect the nation" (p. 79). Stated more simply, such images of the American everyman through the sport of NASCAR and through constructed stories of Pat Tillman's patriotism and bravery situated a White man as the very essence of America and its traditional values. As the media used these Whitened sporting spaces and heroes to tell patriotic, nationalist stories, they practiced exclusion on the basis of race, class, gender, and sexuality—anyone who was not the White everyman could not fully represent the American nation. Even though they were expressly meant to unify and heal, many of these uses of sport actually exacerbated existing divisions in U.S. society.

Sport and Globalization

As you ponder sport and the current global era, recognize that processes of **globalization** are not new and that this long-term historical process actually exhibits multiple disjunctures or contact points that do not quite fit like well-worn puzzle pieces (Sage, 2010). In fact, many social scientists suggest that in order to understand globalization in any era, we must be willing to observe more than the flow of capital or finances, and we must imagine global entanglements beyond a tidy progress story. Global flows are messy, and by their very nature they interrupt, contribute,

globalization—The process that ideas, products, and culture undergo to result in their international integration.

OLYMPICS AND PARALYMPICS

The modern Olympic Games began in 1896 and included no female participants. Women were admitted into the Games in 1900 in a limited number of sports, though their numbers grew slowly. By 1976 at the Summer Games in Montreal, women still did not make up 20 percent of the participating athletes. Compare this to the 2012 Summer Games in London. These Games marked the first time in Olympic history that every national Olympic committee included a female athlete in their delegation! Muslim countries (including Saudi Arabia, which had until then refused to include women) finally relented. Moreover, for the first time ever, the United States delegation had more female athletes than male athletes. However, this was achieved in part because the women's soccer team qualified for the Games and the men's team did not. Had the men's team qualified, there would have been more male athletes in

Although women have been participating as athletes in the Olympics for more than 100 years, the participation representation of women in both athletic and governing positions is still low.

the delegation. And although some sports include the same number of female and male participants, like basketball (12 teams, 144 athletes for both), some sports are still inequitable, such as boxing, which offers male athletes nine weight classes, while women have three. Gender equity in the Paralympic Games is much worse: Some sports are not offered to women (soccer) and some sports are designated as coed, with minimal numbers of female participants (wheelchair rugby includes 3 women among 90-plus male athletes).

1. What factors would allow for a country to be more inclusive of women on the Olympic and Paralympic delegation?

2. What factors would allow for a sport (and consider Winter Games sports) to be more inclusive of women?

3. Despite the improvements in numbers of female competitors, the low percentage of women as sport leaders in the IOC, national governing bodies, and sport governing bodies (few exceed 20 percent female participation) indicate that progress at administrative levels remains slow. What factors might improve the numbers of women included in sport organizations and leadership?

and alter various local flows (Appadurai, 1990). In fact, social scientists who study sport and physical activity suggest that globalizing processes are never complete but rather are always partial, and they simultaneously invite cooperation as well as conflict, sameness and difference, inclusion and exclusion, order and disorder, and liberation as much as control (Robertson, 1992). So, you may be asking how processes of globalization matter in sport settings. Surely, you already have some response to this excellent question, since you may have observed efforts by professional sport businesses to either gather talent from around the world or export their product to other locales. You may also know people from beyond North America who wonder why the Olympic Games include the sports they do rather than more "worldly" sports. Keep pondering these sorts of questions, and you will deepen your understanding of sport and globalization.

Recall that throughout this book, readers have been invited to apply a sociological imagination, that is, a perspective that considers social structures, dominant cultural ideas, and historical influences. Thinking about globalization requires a focus on each of these three aspects of all societies. For example, after the World Wars during what we refer to as the postcolonial era, difference and identity became more fluid and less tied to geography—that is, people may have ties to lands in which they do not maintain a home. For sociologists, this raises questions about the meaning of nation in a global era. Much of Bairner's research reveals that globalizing processes do not necessarily remove ties or value for the nation but rather may create new social spaces in which the nation and the world are in contact toward new cultural understandings, economic relations, and political ideas. Similarly, George Sage (2010) offers an overview of the ways that social scientists have tried to make sense of these national, international, and global interactions.

For example, in sport contexts, people may root for their national team, even if that team includes members who are not from that nation. As well, the presence of sport clubs (in particular, new settlement communities, such as Latino communities in the U.S. Midwestern states) may serve not only to integrate newcomers to their host culture but also to alter the local context for all members of the locale. Juan Pescador (2004) explained this through his historiography of soccer and boxing clubs in Chicago and Detroit. Pescador's research revealed the ways that seemingly exclusive forms of community building through participation in sport clubs actually reflect processes of creolization, or mixing in ways that integrate difference rather than remove it, and transnationality. In the case of the United States and Mexico, community building through sport may create new spaces for dual allegiances to the nation. Pescador wrote that "in the soccer fields a transnational and transborder community emerges from the interaction between Mexican traditions and American values" (p. 371). As a source of **transnational** identity, unlike the formal national requirements of either the Mexican or U.S. governing bodies, the soccer field creates the possibility for new forms of membership in a newly imagined world. Thus, questions about global sport as creating either sameness or difference may actually be too simple for the worlds in which we live. Perhaps more relevant questions will get at the various ways that sporting spaces participate in the complex global shifts and contours of our highly mobile social worlds.

transnational—Crossing international borders to include both or many countries.

 **CHIEN-MING WANG IN MLB**

Taiwanese baseball player Chien-Ming Wang joined MLB's New York Yankees in 2005. Chen (2012) examined the various narratives of the New York Yankees in the Taiwanese media when Wang was on the team and after his departure. Chen found nationalistic themes connecting the New York Yankees to Taiwanese national identity when Wang played for the team but saw this nationalism dissipate once Wang left the team. More than 20,000 articles appeared in a variety of Taiwanese newspapers related to the New York Yankees between 2005, when Wang signed with the team, and 2011, when he was released. Initially, Taiwan celebrated the New York team and claimed the Yankees as their national team. As Wang experienced injuries and his relationship with the team shifted, eventually leading to his release, the Taiwanese media shifted toward a narrative of the Yankees as the "Evil Empire."

1. Have you noticed similar insider–outsider affiliations with sport by other nations?

2. Do you and your family and friends have varied nationalist affiliations with sport teams?

3. At which sporting events do you feel that these nationalist ties most show up? Why?

The World Baseball Classic (WBC) is a terrific example of the influences and results of globalization. Created by MLB and other professional leagues around the world, the WBC was first organized in 2005 as an international baseball tournament. At the most recent WBC, the competition was won by the Dominican Republic, whose team was led by then New York Yankee Robinson Canó. The major league all-star's participation for his home country illustrates the global flows of labor migration: Many of MLB's top players represented their home countries in the tournament, and the American team did not fare well in competition, indicating that much of MLB's talent is not born and bred in the United States. How many of the players on your favorite team played for another country? How many countries are represented by the roster of your favorite team?

Professional soccer is another sport that illustrates the migration of labor, with players from all over the world playing for teams located far from their origins. These players might then return "home" to represent their country in the World Cup or Olympic tournament.

Another consideration for social scientists who study sport in globalization is the role of elite athletes as transnational or migrant laborers and as cosmopolitan citizens. Sporting laborers, or athletes who are paid for their athletic labor, may be considered migrant laborers like any others. For example, Mike Giardina (2005) examined the global appeal of Swiss tennis player Martina Hingis (who was born in Slovakia and also has Czech nationality). His analysis suggested that in addition to being an elite tennis athlete whose skills drew crowds around the world, Hingis enjoyed a cosmopolitan citizenship. In this sense, "cosmopolitan citizenship" refers to Hingis' transnational identity, including multilingual skills, cultural knowledge in various locales, and, most important, the ways that these attributes interacted with a global market for elite sport to create a less-bordered lived experience for her. Yes, like you, Martina Hingis has a home country (Switzerland) and a nationalist identity, yet her financial and cultural ability to move around the world created the conditions of her cosmopolitan citizenship, much like the sporting nationalism that Bairner described.

Sociologists of sport have also studied major sport celebrities such as David Beckham as well as lesser-known itinerant athlete laborers such as young footballers in development leagues (Elliot & Weedon, 2011), athletes hoping to be drafted into MLB from Latin baseball leagues (Klein, 2006), Korean athletes on the U.S. LPGA tour (Lim, 2009; Shin & Nam, 2004), and urban youth involved in "lifestyle sports" in post-apartheid South Africa (Wheaton, 2013). Each of these analyses suggests that sport plays a crucial role in the economic and professional development of many athletes, not only the most celebrated ones. These analyses often unveil demanding and even dangerous paths from amateur to professional athlete status and shine a light on the cultural influence of transnational sport venues and celebrities on more local engagements in sport.

You may have noticed that studies of sport and globalization tend to focus on male experiences of economic aspects of globalization. However, some sociologists of sport have brought analyses of gender into the global equation. For example, several scholars have described the role of Aboriginal Australian runner Cathy Freeman in drawing attention to an Australian legacy of racial inequality and ongoing need for Aboriginal rights. The analyses of Freeman reveal the ways the popular media exploited her politically, highlighting her lighter complexion, preferred feminine attractiveness, and Aboriginal identity in order to depict more politically demanding Aboriginal activists as unpatriotic (Gardiner, 2003). Regardless of how the mass media depicted her, Freeman often disrupted the official Australian citizenship narrative by running her victory laps draped in the Aboriginal flag as well as the Australian flag. Much like the black-gloved raised fists of Olympians Tommie Smith and John Carlos in 1968, Freeman's flag-draped Black Australian body came to represent the difficult racist policies that were part of Australia's colonial relations

 Quick Fact

Sugar is a 2008 film that chronicles the fictional experiences of Dominican player Miguel Santos in the American minor league baseball system. In the film, Santos faces isolation and struggles in his quest to stay in baseball. Eventually, the pitcher leaves the team but remains in the United States to see if he is able to find another way to achieve the American dream and help his impoverished family in his home country. The sport drama, although fiction, was a stark reminder of the economics of professional baseball and the amount of money MLB teams spend to recruit and sign cheap talent from Latin American countries as well as the way the MLB then sees these players as expendable commodities when they do not succeed.

⭐ SUSAN BIRRELL, PROFESSOR, UNIVERSITY OF IOWA

Susan Birrell is a faculty member at the University of Iowa. As an undergraduate, Dr. Birrell attended St. Lawrence University in upstate New York. She participated on the school's sport teams before Title IX. Dr. Birrell attended graduate school at the University of Massachusetts at Amherst during the 1970s, a time period at UMass that produced some leading scholars in the field of sport studies. One of Birrell's classmates at UMass was Peter Donnelly, another Success Story subject. Birrell was hired at the University of Iowa and led their sport studies program, which now resides in the university's American studies program. Her scholarship has helped shape the ways sport sociologists think and write about gender and race. Equally important, Birrell has influenced sport scholars in the field who attended Iowa, including Mary McDonald, Georgia Tech University; Rita Liberti, California State University at East Bay; Sarah Fields, University of Denver; Dan Nathan, Skidmore College; Shelley Lucas, Boise State University; Laura Chase, Cal Poly Pomona; Theresa Walton, Kent State University; and Jaime Schultz, Penn State.

Photo courtesy of Susan Birrell.

with Britain. One may observe some of these gendered, ethnic exploitations by watching the opening ceremonies of the 2000 Sydney Summer Games.

Corporate Nationalism

Sociologists of sport are also interested in exploring the alignment between corporate media and sport and the globalization of sporting brands. The NFL and the NBA represent what Maguire (2005) referred to as sporting brands and also as sporting transnational corporations. Many conversations of globalization, it seems, often return to a dualism of homogeneity versus heterogeneity, but Maguire's work reminds us that this is a much too simplistic characterization of the space, place, and flow of global sport. So, we are challenged to see how the local and global are constantly engaged in a dance of sorts and acknowledge an intermingling of the two that produces what some scholars have referred to as the "glocal." Yet a corporate nationalism at times exercises exploitative power and may use folkways or nationalist ethnic traditions to sell or authenticate a national identity.

Corporate nationalism, for social scientists, reflects the manner in which for-profit corporate structures come to represent and, at times, exercise power to cogovern the nation. In sport studies, studies of corporate nationalism have focused on the cultural power of multinational corporations,

corporate nationalism—The ways that for-profit corporate structures come to represent and, at times, exercise power to cogovern the nation.

like Nike, to rhetorically construct ideas about good citizenship through engagement in the right forms of physical activity. So, while you may be well aware of Nike's invitation to you and all your friends to "just do it," you are less likely to be familiar with the Surgeon General's call for adults to exercise for at least 150 minutes per week (U.S. Department of Health and Human Services, 2010).

The fact that Nike's message gets out more easily and recognizably than does that of the nation's top doctor marks Nike's power to promote their brand of American nationalism. At the same time, Nike's messages also work to brand you, the consumer, as a Nike-wearing, regularly exercising "good" American. For example, in 2008, Nike hosted a global unifying physical activity event, The Human Race, in which 780,000 runners were estimated to have participated either on their own or as part of a hosted 10K in their home community (Ronca, 2010). The event purportedly celebrated and united runners all over the world, but of course also did so through the company's Nike+ products, which offer a digital space for sharing running data. In some ways, we might say this event most notably unified Nike devotees or customers.

Of course, Nike is not the only perpetrator of sport-related corporate nationalism—there are too many examples to cover in this brief chapter, but we will offer a couple more. Have you ever participated in a cause-related run, bike ride, or walk? Perhaps you or your friends have done the Avon 39 or participated in the NFL Play60 program? These are also examples of corporate nationalism and likely are related to something Samantha King referred to as "global strategic corporate philanthropy and community relations," or GSCR (2005, p. 84). GSCR represents a formal strategy among transnational corporations to read their local profit centers and represent themselves as caring, present, and invested in the specific needs of the local community. These sorts of corporate practices emerge in a moment when corporations feel the need to perform a local sensibility as they simultaneously collude in the disappearance of local small businesses.

King's careful study of the Avon corporation's GSCR offers original interview data as well as mediated messaging and annual reports regarding the Avon Worldwide Fund for Women's Health and the Avon Running Global Women's Circuit. King investigated the gendered nature of transnational corporate marketing as well as the intentional use of sport events by corporations unrelated to sport to create new spaces of global consumer appeal. One message from King's analyses is that sport matters in global business strategizing. More important, she argued that we must take seriously the ways that sport and narratives of corporate responsibility get used to veil or soften the increasing levels of power offered to transnational corporations in defining societal needs and crafting oversimplified, falsely universalized responses. One recent example is the NFL's use of "pink" campaigns—wearing pink uniforms, adding pink to the field—to link their corporation to efforts to fight breast cancer.

In yet another example, Steve Jackson and Brendan Hokowhitu (2005) studied the process of global economic and media expansion of what was then called the New Zealand Rugby Football Union (NZRFU; now known as New Zealand Rugby). Interestingly, both the sport of rugby and the indigenous Maori culture are central to New Zealand national identity. The NZRFU partnered with the athletic apparel company Adidas in order to gain much-needed global exposure and financial backing. Jackson and Hokowhitu found that NZRFU appropriated the Maori tradition of the haka, their traditional ancestral war cry or dance, as a preevent ritual to bolster fan connections to both New Zealand nationalism and traditional Maori culture. They also reported that despite significant visibility in certain sports, especially rugby, Maori community members continue to face economic, political, and cultural marginalization in many ways in New Zealand. In fact, Maori leaders were not formally consulted regarding the use of the haka for the NZRFU or for a subsequent advertisement developed by Adidas.

What is crucial for our understanding of sport and globalization is that a corporate nationalism was believed to be in the best interest of all New Zealanders because it would increase global interest in their national sport and highlight indigenous culture of the nation. As you know, in today's swiftly moving cultural terrain, many formerly sacred moments and events frequently get shared through social media. Therefore, as Jackson and Hokowhitu's research indicates, it becomes challenging for indigenous communities to claim ownership of their rituals. In this case, Adidas made a global spectacle of the haka before protests led to questions about ownership and called for a review of the emergent links between global capitalism, new media technologies, and transnational advertising. Once again, the role of sport in nationalist agendas was clear.

The Short of It

- Sport of the nation illuminates the ways that sport emerges in all nations as a reflection of the historical, political, and cultural conditions of the nation.
- Sport for the nation focuses on the ways that sporting practices reflect national beliefs, and sporting events offer a national and world stage in which to assert nationalist ideas.
- Globalization is not a new phenomenon and actually has been a factor in the development of sporting nationalisms for many years.
- Sporting nationalism refers to personal connections through sporting teams or sports in general and includes analyses of the role of sport in the development of national identities.
- Corporate sporting nationalism refers to the role of sport in the global strategizing of transnational corporations and the belief that corporate sport entities serve the nation well.

CHAPTER 7

Sport and Physical Activity in Societal Change

In this chapter you will learn the following:

✓ How the sociological study of sport and physical activity contributes to a better society

✓ The engagement of sport and physical activity in social movements

✓ The goals of sport for development

✓ Ideas for advocacy for a physically active society

✓ How to remain engaged in sociological study of sport and physical activity

---

> We use soccer to teach a curriculum of life and job skills.
>
> **Lawrence Cann**, Street Soccer USA

By now, you are well versed in the crucial role of sport and physical activity in everyday life. At this point, it ought to be difficult to observe human physical culture, whether it be leisure, elite competition, or exercise, without thinking about the societal structural, cultural, and historical legacies that influence that human movement. This is a gift from your social scientist friends to you! While it may seem exhausting at times, you now have an increased capacity to make sense of the social world you inhabit, which will also help you imagine yourself as an architect in this social world. Moreover, you now have some tools that enable you to creatively put physical activity to use toward addressing current social issues and problems.

Really, at a basic level, human movement has always been central to social movements and social change. When you think of major social movements, try to recall one where the human body and human movement were not central. Recall, for example, the French Revolution with its call to storm the Bastille or the U.S. civil rights movement with its many marches, bus boycotts, walkouts, and sit-ins at previously segregated spaces. The human body and human movement were central in these moments of social change. More recently, in the **Occupy movement**, marches and an embodied reclamation of public spaces through tent communities marked key aspects of the movement. For many sociologists of sport, embodiment and human movement are clearly central to social change, and it is important to apply a sociological perspective to questions about the role of sport and physical activity in processes of addressing societal-level issues.

Occupy movement—An international movement protesting social and economic inequality. One of its primary goals was to make the economic and political relations in all societies less vertically hierarchical and more flatly, evenly distributed.

In this chapter, we return to the underlying logic of the sociological imagination, especially as it relates to the role of sport and physical activity in societal-level change. At its core, the sociological imagination requires people to develop the capacity to make sense of both their own biography and the social conditions they inherit. In other words, one must be willing and able to identify personal troubles as always already linked with broader public issues. For example, when you cannot gather enough friends to play a pickup baseball game in your neighborhood, it is not so much about your availability of friends as it is about the increase in highly organized leagues and lack of publicly available play space. Even if you really enjoy your neighborhood friends, it is likely that your parents are more inclined to enroll you in a centralized organized baseball league than to simply encourage you to organize yourselves in a nearby public park. In fact, in many U.S. neighborhoods today, that park is unlikely to exist.

Not surprisingly, C. Wright Mills (1959/2004) promoted this type of everyday sociological imagining as a necessary response to one's role in a rapidly changing social world. Like Mills, most social scientists would argue that social structures are

 TRANSGENDER ATHLETES AND LEAGUES

Traditionally, sport has been categorized in a binary fashion, with separate teams for male and female players. With the growing inclusion of transgender athletes, leagues and sport organizations are fashioning policies to determine and establish which teams are accessible to transgender athletes as well as form policies about when these athletes can begin participation (related to their transition).

Travers and Deri (2010) provide an overview of lesbian softball leagues. Many started in the 1970s as an alternative to the homophobic space of women's sport teams and the sexism of coed leagues (including gay coed teams). Lesbian softball leagues' inclusion of transgender athletes has been mixed. To examine the response of these leagues, Travers and Deri interviewed 12 transgender athletes who had played on a lesbian softball team in the two years prior. Among the 12 subjects were 8 FTM (female to male) trans men, 3 MTF (male to female) trans women, and 1 genderqueer/trans lesbian. Their initial conclusion viewed the lesbian softball teams as being welcoming to the participants most of the time. The three MTF trans women all reported that their leagues were welcoming and their participation felt empowering. The FTM trans men reported mixed experiences, receiving comments that ranged from welcoming to hostile. The men concluded that many of their opponents were unfamiliar with the league's trans policy and that other teams found out about the policy only because of the men's participation. Still, they all reported being encouraged and supported, usually by teammates or coaches. One trans man was asked by other players why he wanted to be identified as "a he" while playing in a league for women. Another felt he was being punished by lesbians for transitioning. Interview segments provided illustration for how issues of trans awareness, the role of testosterone, and the inclusion of trans men are discussed.

1. How does the inclusion of trans athletes in team sport reveal the need to make changes in the ways we organize sport using the gender binary?

2. Would such changes be more accepted in adult sport leagues, such as the one described by Travers and Deri?

3. Or could we expect such changes to occur at younger levels of sport as more children identify as trans?

constantly changing, yet people are always trying to find stability in these dynamic social spaces. For many of us, it is within this rapid and ongoing societal-level change that we may observe the role of sport and physical activity in both advancing change and offering stability to masses of people as they attempt to make sense of the social conditions they have inherited. To consistently operate from this core stage of the sociological imagination where we are able to understand our personal experiences as broader societal issues, we must understand processes of social change and, specifically, the role of sport and physical activity in such change.

Types of Social Change in Sport and Physical Activity

For sociologists, **social change** is any alteration in the cultural, structural, population, or ecological characteristics of a social system. Recall that sociologists are interested in systems and their parts (or societal structures) and in ideas and beliefs that inform, maintain, or change this structure (also known as dominant culture or ideology).

Sociologist Jay Coakley (2009, p. 564) suggested that a "conservative" goal of growth is most common among people involved in sport. For some, a primary interest may be the "reformist" goal of improvement. Other folks who are invested in sport seek a "radical" goal of transformation. Building on Coakley's insights, a goal of growth in sport may indeed emerge from conservative and market-driven interests as well as from a fundamental belief that sport is a good, well-functioning component of society. So why not increase its size and influence? When we consider sport for its more complex link to broad societal-level inequalities such as poverty, sexism, racism, and ableism, we move into the reformist stage of goals, even if growth is a component of the goal. For example, to some extent, Title IX (the U.S. law requiring gender equity in federally funded educational settings) seeks growth of sport, but it does so within a set of policies that bring sport into a more gender-equitable, ethical context as it plays its role in the educational system for all citizens. As Coakley suggested, improvement of sport and physical activity is often a well-supported goal, but there is often quite a range of priorities for specific reforms. Finally, to view a sport-focused, radical goal of transformation, we return to our example of the dismantling of apartheid mentioned throughout the book.

Quick Fact

Changes in community design and labor force participation are related to most people's access to healthy food. Your neighbors who participate in the Supplemental Nutritional Assistance Program may have to travel farther than you to find a grocery store willing to accept their state-sponsored food support vouchers. Imagine trying to exercise regularly while worried about your next meal (Ver Ploeg, Mancino, Todd, Clay, & Scharadin, 2015).

Recall that there were many moments where athletes, in concert with political leaders, called for changes in major sport organizations that would eventually lead to a dismantling of the socially unjust racial hierarchy that existed in South Africa. While the goal was to end apartheid, the process also brought attention to racism as it existed in sport governing bodies, like the IOC and the International Tennis Federation. To the extent that this broad social movement sought policy and structural change in sport governing bodies to not endorse apartheid, their aims became a radical, transformative set of goals for broad societal change.

> **social change**—Any alteration in the cultural, structural, population, or ecological characteristics of a social system.

Apartheid was a policy of enforced racial registration and segregation that created a false hierarchy between the White and Black communities of South Africans. Let's quickly observe three moments where global attention to apartheid was central at a major sporting event. First, in the 1968 Summer Olympic Games, the Olympic Human Rights Project was guided by a set of social justice demands, one of which was the exclusion of South Africa from the Games to bring attention to their policy of apartheid. Second, in 1969, Arthur Ashe, African American and number one–ranked tennis player in the United States at the time, was denied a travel visa by the South African government, based on their policy of apartheid. Arthur Ashe took this opportunity to recognize his seemingly individual problem into a public issue and began seeking international support for boycott of South African tennis. In 1973, Ashe was granted a visa. Under great scrutiny, he traveled to South Africa and played tennis as a free Black man. In some ways, by participating in the South African tournament, he was supporting the racially divided nation. Yet by demonstrating that a Black man ought to have equal rights and opportunities under the law, he brought a great deal of symbolic power to the fight against apartheid. Perhaps the most well-known example is how the 1995 Rugby World Cup, hosted by a post-apartheid

 DAVE ZIRIN, JOURNALIST

Dave Zirin is not your average sportswriter. He doesn't attend sporting events and provide a synopsis of the game with statistics. Instead, Zirin is more interested in examining the various political issues in sport, or, as he states, the place where sports and politics collide. Zirin publishes a regular column on his website, www.edgeofsports.com, and his writings appear in *The Nation* and sometimes on the websites of *ESPN* and *Grantland*. His most recent book, *Brazil's Dance With the Devil: The World Cup, the Olympics, and the Fight for Democracy* (2014) examines Rio de Janeiro, the host city for the 2014 World Cup and 2016 Summer Olympic Games, and the various political issues endemic to hosting mega-events. His recent columns have focused on gay athletes in sports, ethics of professional sport team owners, the relationship between immigration reform and sport, concussions, and Nelson Mandela's use of sport in South African politics. While not trained in sport sociology, Zirin is an ally, and his writings provide alternative perspectives rarely found in American mainstream media.

South Africa, became a symbol of a newly unified nation under the leadership of President Nelson Mandela, the country's first Black president. Through these three examples, one can see the political power of sport—both at the biographical level, as it inspired particular participants to seek more ethical agreements among nations, and at the societal level, as policies over time created a set of conditions that made the ending of apartheid a productive change for the nation.

Taking this conversation a bit further, consider nonsport forms of physical activity, which have been part and parcel of societal change and affect numerous members of society in more direct ways than elite sport does. Currently, one can easily observe a conservative growth goal around physical activity in the moral obligation to exercise more and weigh less. Employer-sanctioned physical activity programs and even a resurgence in free or low-cost community physical activity programs are not necessarily bad things, but our sociological imagination leads us to ask about broader societal-level issues like access to health care and safe, affordable food as well as the ethics of setting health insurance rates based on preexisting conditions. A reformist goal of improvement would address the inequalities mentioned previously and ensure that new community physical activity programs are actually accessible to all. The radical goal of transformation would be more broadly focused on creating a society that is physically active and nutritionally resourced in equitable ways. For example, a reduction in reliance on cars could make current highway, road, and parking lot spaces available for other uses and would immediately increase physical activity among a majority of members of society. Programs such as Open Streets help people envision such a society by making this a reality in particular communities on a monthly basis.

The Open Streets Project is a collaboration between two public action groups that promote more people-friendly and activity-friendly use of urban streets. Together, the Alliance for Biking and Walking and the Street Plans Collaborative work toward a goal of creating more nonmotorized use of urban streets through sharing information, highlighting strategies, and supporting the growth of Open Streets programs across North America. The Open Streets Project offers a published guide and an interactive website, allowing advocates and new Open Streets organizers to explore efforts in other peer cities as well as to track how people might choose to use urban streets if they were not constantly used only for motorized traffic. The Open Streets Project, then, is at once an online and on-the-ground social movement to reduce North American reliance on motorized transport and to return urban streets to the people, who may then more freely choose to be physically active throughout their daily activities.

 Sport can no longer be considered a luxury within any society but is an important investment in the present and future, particularly in developing countries.

United Nations Office on Sport for Development and Peace

Sport Development and Sport for Development

One of the most important and exciting areas of research around sport and social change is development. Of course, if you are a kinesiologist, you ought to believe in the potential of daily physical activity to enhance quality of life, yet you also ought to have a healthy skepticism about the power of sport to enhance lives on its own. In fact, the research on sport for youth development suggests that an overzealous belief in the righteousness of sport and physical activity may actually limit the potential of program outcomes. As Coakley (2011) indicated in his review of research on sport programs for youth development, an unquestioning belief in sport programs as protective, cleansing, or inspirational leads to limited program goal setting and skewed outcome evaluations.

Imagine your friend joined a skateboard club and her brother did not. Now, imagine that both of them did well in school, graduated with honors from college, and found well-paying, enjoyable work as adults. In this case, can we say that the skateboarding program saved your friend from otherwise poor choices, or that it cleansed her from the negative forces in broader society, or that it created the possibility for her success? According to Coakley's review, much more evidence is needed about the ways that sport and physical activity programs link with other social resources not only to advance individual quality of life but also to improve whole communities. In fact, he suggested that sport and physical activity programs are actually undermined when not carefully considered for their potential to link with other forms of civic engagement. Such programs cannot only be about the physical—they must always also be considered for the ways they are deeply tied to cultural, social, political, and civic engagements among participants.

Related to such questions about the role of sport and physical activity programs for youth development is a more global industry of sport development and sport for development and peace. Former United Nations Secretary Kofi Annan once suggested that we must see "sport as a means to promote education, health, development and peace" (2004). Considering the role of sport in international movements for development is also of interest to sociologists of sport and physical activity.

In his work on sport for peace and development, Simon Darnell (2010) historicized the concept of **developmentalism**, linking it to President Truman's 1949 inaugural address where Truman spoke of the need for economic, social, and political improvements in the world's "underdeveloped areas." More specifically, Truman called for northern, democratic, and "developed" nations to commit to increasing opportunity for production and prosperity for the world's poor. This was an important moment in global development while the major powers were redefining the meaning and purpose of nation as self-ruled, rational (e.g., meaning based in European ideas of science as opposed to other forms of knowledge), and progress

developmentalism—A body of political economic thought that advocates state-managed markets in the national interest and aims to reflect the needs of late industrializing nations so that they may "catch up" with more advanced capitalist economies. This economic perspective emerged in reaction to global economic inequality and unchecked Western economic and political power.

oriented (desire to develop infrastructure and free-market economies that resembled those of developed nations). Truman's address and the policy and governance structures that were developed in response to his call are now considered the genesis of developmentalism, or a movement to stabilize a world economy through a three-part process of promoting the following:

- An essentialist view of the "developing world" and its members as a homogenous group
- An unyielding belief in progress and the modernization of society
- A centrality of the nation-state as a focal point and leading participant in the development process

As a way to rebuild society, developmentalism failed in many cases. Some argue that it increased the gap between developed nations and developing nations while simultaneously generating a host of caricatures of nations that couldn't quite get it together the way their developed siblings did (Darnell, 2010). Yet Darnell argued that to the extent that sport is uncritically used in alignment with modernist or neoliberal goals of developmentalism, its potential for creating real change and addressing real societal problems will be diminished. In fact, sport may become part of the hierarchy of global relations in development projects.

Sport may also be intentionally used as a means for addressing developmental societal needs. For example, in 2013, the UN General Assembly approved the proclamation of an International Day of Sport for Development and Peace. This proclamation marked long-standing commitments by both the IOC and the UN on various projects featuring sport as tool for social change. In fact, since 2009, the IOC has held UN observer status ("UN Creates International Day," 2013), which means that as an organization, the IOC has the right to speak at UN General Assembly meetings—a powerful global platform for expressing ideas. To be clear, the IOC does not have voting privileges, which suggests there is a limit to their power and privilege through their observer status. Still, the message is clear: Sport is considered a meaningful component of any array of developmental tools and strategies for building and rebuilding society.

Process of Social Change

Beyond the basic social science definition offered earlier, the process of social change invites an engagement in the scholarly and practical task of challenging conventional wisdom and working toward social, economic, and environmental justice. Although the promise of a better world is implicit in the notion of social change, we recognize the difficulties and complexities associated with these efforts and the questions they raise about how intentions to do good bear out in practice. Current movements for social change bear the legacy of past ones, thus requiring us to

Brown v. Board of Education— The 1954 U.S. Supreme Court decision that outlawed segregation in public education by finding that separate public schools for Blacks and Whites were inherently unequal and therefore unconstitutional.

understand the functioning and implications of contemporary relationships of power and politics in specific contexts as well as to reimagine alternative and more just societal relationships.

Industrialization, the Civil Rights Bill, and emergent reliance on oil are all examples of social change. In order for social change to occur, there typically needs to be some redistribution of power. Although social systems are always in the process of change, it takes a good amount of time to effect real systemic change, especially like those changes mentioned previously. We tend to recall moments like ***Brown v. Board of Education*** (1954), which unanimously held that the racial segregation of children in public schools violated the Equal Protection Clause of the Fourteenth Amendment of the U.S. Constitution, as singular moments of great social change, but such change cannot be reduced to a single moment. In fact, the *Brown v. Board* decision came about after several local legal actions and protests about racial segregation in U.S. public schools. In sport, a great example of this is Title IX. If we locate women's liberation through sport in the 1972 passage of the law, we miss the importance of all the organizing and social movement processes that led to the law as well as the vast cultural change that occurred after implementation of the law.

 RACE, ACTIVISM, AND CONSUMPTION

Cunningham and Regan (2011) examined White consumers' reactions to African American athlete endorsers. Subjects ($N = 73$) were asked to respond to a fictitious African American male Olympian selling a New Balance sneaker. The athlete endorsers varied in terms of volunteer activities they were involved in (either Stop the War Coalition or the Obesity Society) and in terms of their racial identity. Cunningham and Regan were interested to see how White consumers perceived the trustworthiness of the athlete endorsers depending on their political involvement and racial identity. They found that the type of activism and level of racial identity did not have direct effects, but they did influence the consumers' perceptions of trustworthiness. The African American athlete perceived to be the most trustworthy spokesman had a high racial identity and was involved in fighting childhood obesity. They concluded that an athlete's involvement in political activism did not detract from their trustworthiness as a product endorser and suggested that corporations and teams might overstate the case against activism. Despite these findings, in 2013 Chris Kluwe (White), former punter for the Minnesota Vikings, claimed he was released from the team for his outspoken support for marriage equality.

1. Is there a political cause an athlete is affiliated with that would influence you to not purchase the product?

2. Conversely, would the efforts of an athlete to work for a social or political cause encourage you to become more involved and engaged?

Four Stages of Social Movements

One of the earliest scholars to study social movement processes was Herbert Blumer, who identified four stages in the life cycle of social movements: social ferment, popular excitement, formalization, and institutionalization (De la Porta & Diani, 2006). Since his early work, scholars have refined and renamed these stages, but the underlying themes have remained relatively constant. Today, the four social movement stages are often referred to as emergence, coalescence, bureaucratization, and decline. Just to be clear, decline must be understood not as negative but as a part of the evolution of the movement. Scholars have noted that social movements may decline for several reasons and have identified five ways they do decline. These are success, organizational failure, co-optation, repression, and establishment within mainstream society (Macionis, 2001; Miller, 1999). Therefore, a process of coming into being, consensus on societal needs, links with existing social structures and resources, and then a different or reduced need for the specific organized movement collectively constitute a process for social change.

Sport became a crucial, even if largely symbolic, space for global attention to social justice issues in several celebrated moments. In the United States, Jackie Robinson's entry to MLB is heralded as significant moment in the racial civil rights movement. The 1972 tennis match between Billie Jean King and Bobby Riggs was similarly heralded along the gender-related civil rights movement. More recently, the entry of Oscar Pistorius in the Olympic Games as an athlete with a disability shifted our view of able-bodied and disabled athletes. One example where we may apply our sociological imagination to see the threads of social change is in the dismantling of South Africa's policy of apartheid. It encompasses both global issues of race relations and the link between biography and societal conditions.

 Quick Fact

Themed runs are increasing in popularity around the globe, reflecting shifting meanings of and desires for public physical activity. The Color Run held its first event in January 2012, quickly spreading to 50 cities and signing up 600,000 participants. Just one year later, it held events in 120 U.S. cities and 30 countries, with an estimated 1 million runners. The zombie-themed Run for Your Lives held its first race in 2011 and held 20 races for 150,000 participants in 2013. The obstacle series called Tough Mudder started with 3 races in 2010 and expanded to include 53 events worldwide in 2013. Rock 'n' Roll Marathons, which feature race courses lined with bands and cheer squads, operated just 5 races in 2007 and increased to 30 by 2013, including 5 in Europe (Kurtzleben, 2013).

⭐ SAMANTHA KING, PROFESSOR, QUEEN'S UNIVERSITY

Samantha King is a professor at Queen's University in Kingston, Ontario. Her research interests vary, and she has been featured in publications on queer athletes, racial politics, and consumer-oriented breast cancer philanthropy. Her 2006 book, *Pink Ribbons, Inc.: Breast Cancer Culture and the Politics of Philanthropy*, was made into a documentary, an exciting development for any academic! The 2011 film *Pink Ribbons, Inc.* was produced by the National Film Board of Canada. It received wide acclaim, as did the book. King's book argues that the use of pink ribbons and breast cancer runs as fundraising efforts obfuscates the minimal amount of monies raised that actually go toward cancer research. In fact, many of the companies that produce drugs to prolong a cancer patient's life also manufacture products with carcinogen-containing agents. The book and film provide a grounded perspective in examining current practices in body politics.

© Taylor Studios

Sport and Physical Activity Advance Social Change

By now, it ought to be obvious that sport and physical activity are not merely fun and games—they are core elements of social structures and societal belief systems. History includes numerous examples of moments when sport and physical activity became crucial elements in broader social movements. In fact, it is likely that anyone reading this book has participated in a physical activity that was directly affiliated with some larger social issue or movement such as a CROP Walk, AIDS dance-a-thon, Open Streets event, or Race for the Cure. Consider what you learned, how you felt participating in these events, and, most important, how you might now apply your emergent sociological imagination to these experiences. The following section offers examples of social change occurring or unfolding in particular sport contexts. What do these events tell you about societal structures, dominant ideas, and historical contexts?

1965 American Football League All-Star Game Relocated

In January 1965, the American Football League (AFL) All-Star Game was set to be hosted in New Orleans, a city interested in acquiring their own professional football team. When several of the African American all-stars arrived in the southern city, they found themselves confronted with various acts of racism. The group of African American football players met in a hotel room and decided to boycott the game unless it were relocated to another city that was more welcoming. In just a few days,

AFL Commissioner Joe Foss was able to arrange for the game to be relocated to Houston, to the dismay of the New Orleans committee and the celebration of the players who had joined together as a collective to demand change. In the midst of the civil rights movement and legislative efforts to enact changes for African Americans, the action of the African American all-stars marked one of the first times athletes joined together to demand change.

Summer Games of 1968: Olympic Project for Human Rights

The summer of 1968 marked a significant athlete-led movement to meet several social justice goals. Led primarily by Tommie Smith, Lee Evans, and later John Carlos—undergraduate students at San Jose State College and members of the

 ATHLETE ACTIVISM

When Florida teenager Trayvon Martin was murdered, the NBA Miami Heat team, led by LeBron James and Dwyane Wade, posed for photos with the team wearing hoodies in honor of Martin. Several college and professional athletes wore "I Can't Breathe" T-shirts in honor of the last words of Eric Garner, who died when NYPD put him in an illegal chokehold. What examples can you think of that illustrate athlete engagement in social issues?

AP Photo/Kathy Willens/Press Association

Cleveland Cavaliers forward LeBron James warms up before an NBA basketball game against the Brooklyn Nets at the Barclays Center in New York.

WOMEN SKI JUMPING IN THE OLYMPICS

For the first time in Olympic history, women competed in ski jumping at the Sochi Olympic Winter Games in 2014. However, women have been participating and competing in ski jumping for more than 100 years. Why has it taken so long for them to be included in the Olympic Games? For many years, IOC members, including members of the Medical Commission, argued that women should not participate in the sport because it would damage their reproductive organs. Others believed the sport to be appropriate for men only. Perhaps others were afraid of the competition women presented to the male ski jumpers. At the site of the 2010 Vancouver Winter Games, though she could not compete, Lindsey Van established the record, jumping 105.5 meters. During the Games, Swiss ski jumper Simon Ammann jumped 108 meters to set a new record, but the results illustrate the comparable skill of the men and women who compete in the sport. In addition to gaining entry into the Olympic Games in ski jumping in the individual normal hill, male ski jumpers participate in the individual large hill and the team large hill as well as the Nordic combined event, which is cross-country skiing followed by ski jumping. Women remain excluded from the Nordic combined event.

men's track team—this movement continues to be a model for resistance and reformative justice. Drawing attention to race relations of the time in both the United States and abroad, the work of these three students unveiled a newly influential social status and role of the athlete as social and political organizer. You probably recall or know of the black-gloved raised fists of Tommie Smith and John Carlos on the Olympic medal stand—a moment immortalized in essays, books, posters, and statues around the world. What do you imagine were the steps in this social movement process that led to the now-immortalized medal stand activism?

The all-too-often missing piece of this story is the longstanding organizing that had been happening before the 1968 Summer Games. In fact, after several organizing meetings, many led by Dr. Harry Edwards, a social movement called the Olympic Project for Human Rights (OPHR) was formed and a set of demands was drafted. The OPHR demands linked the Olympic Games to broad geopolitical issues, especially around globalized racism and structural inequality, and specified an end to apartheid in South Africa, White privilege in the New York Athletic Club and the IOC, and IOC sanctions against those nations that supported such racist policies. This example of social movement is particularly illustrative of the many educational and professional roles in which people participated. Although the Olympic athletes held the most symbolic power during the Games, journalists, educators, coaches, and family members also made this movement possible.

Consider the many ways that such a movement may be supported, especially since we cannot all be the leaders or spokespersons for every social movement we support. As well, consider the process of this social movement, which we know to be a process even though the mass media often reduces such complicated events to a particular moment.

Billie Jean King and Bobby Riggs Tennis Match in 1972

In the same year that Title IX was passed, the nation was still wrestling with the broader societal issues of gender equity in the workplace, home, parenting, and mass media. This broader social movement beyond Title IX was referred to as the women's liberation movement. Throughout this social movement, a varied set of public symbols of change around gender equity and sexist beliefs became useful, such as the burning of bras, marches on Washington D.C., reports on pay inequities, and increasing numbers of lawsuits calling for equity in various publicly funded settings.

Then there was the "battle of the sexes" tennis match between two U.S. professional tennis athletes, Bobby Riggs and Billie Jean King. The event garnered much television and print media attention both in the lead-up and during the event. Based on public commentary, the event clearly held meaning far beyond the tennis court and was deeply tied to the righteous belief in either side of the women's liberation movement. Again, although much political and educational work had been done throughout a broader movement before this tennis match, Billie Jean King's defeat of her male opponent became a powerful symbol of women's capacity to meet and compete with men, if given the chance, in any social role. This change was already occurring in broader society, yet this tennis event further advanced that change by making the new social order of gender equity both accessible and demanding.

The Short of It

- Human movement has always been central to social movements and social change.
- Sport and physical activity play roles in advancing change and offering stability to masses of people as they attempt to make sense of the social conditions they have inherited.
- The growing presence of transgender athletes is leading leagues and sport organizations to fashion policies related to accessibility and equity beyond traditional gender and sex binaries.

- Changes in community design and labor force participation are related to most people's access to healthy food.
- Social change is any alteration in the cultural, structural, population, or ecological characteristics of a social system.
- Sport and physical activity programs cannot only be about the physical; they must always also be considered for the ways they are deeply tied to cultural, social, political, and civic engagements among participants.

Epilogue

The Future of Sociology of Sport and Physical Activity

Surely, reading this book has provoked you to consider the significant role of physical activity throughout our lives as well as the power you hold to create a more meaningful physically active community and society. It has been our goal to invite you into a new and perhaps more expanded understanding of your own involvement in sport and physical activity and that of others you may encounter in your social world. Toward this end, in each chapter we have sought to link broad social conditions, including dominant cultural beliefs, structures of daily interaction, and historical trends, with possible individual experiences. This draws you into the core of the sociological imagination, a perspective that holds great promise for full engagement of societal members, especially when applied to all aspects of our daily encounters, including sport and physical activity. Whether your connections to sport and physical activity emerge out of professional practice, advocacy, or participation, a sociological imagination will aid you in consistently observing, recognizing, and acting in ways that promote healthy, just, and physically active communities.

It is impossible to describe all settings for meaningful sport and physical activity engagement, yet throughout this book, we have invited you to consider elite, profit-oriented forms of sport, highly organized and competitive youth sport, state-sponsored physical education, global sport such as the FIFA World Cup and the Olympic Games, exercise as consumer activity, and neighborhood low-organized sport and physical activity. These diverse settings generate a variety of social, economic, political, and cultural engagements around and through physical activity. As many of the authors cited throughout this text suggest, each of us is the architect of meaningful sport and physical activity programs. This endows us with a certain amount of social power and simultaneously invites us to take full responsibility for the communities we develop and sustain. Taking on this responsibility will require a clarity of mission around justice-oriented sport and physical activity for all societal members across the life span. The sociological imagination will require that your responsibility in this be deeply linked to your ever-growing capacity to consider historical, cultural, and structural components of any community or social world.

By now, it is clear to you that you must consider sport in the 21st century, its cultural meaning, and its social structural components within the historical moment. For example, the current moment is marked by globalization and rapid technological change. More than ever, sport is a global product consumed by an array of people in highly evolved technological ways. Yet, when we exercise and compete in sport, we often experience very basic human emotions and connections to others, including teammates, friends, coaches, and family members. The social world today is also marked by major political, cultural, and social change. Key aspects of sport and physical activity, such as the meaning of winning or striving for a personal record, continue to evolve; some leagues provide a medal for every participant as a means to encourage continued participation, and others selecting only the most elite performers for competition. This post–September 11 era is also marked by a heightened sense of national security. Yet, paradoxically, while we are hyperconcerned with security at sporting events, we sometimes seem less concerned with the personal securities of athletes, including injuries incurred while playing sport.

Attitudes around social issues continue to evolve and change, confronting those in sport with conflicting ways of making sense of the social world. For example, ideas about sex, gender, and sexuality are rapidly changing. In sport in 2014, we saw the Indian runner Dutee Chand disqualified from the Commonwealth Games for having a so-called gender-nonconforming body. That same year, Michael Sam, a U.S. collegiate football athlete, publicly acknowledged his gay identity before the NFL draft, a rare occurrence in men's sports, and was still drafted by an NFL team (though eventually cut). Sport also interacts with changing attitudes about race. When nine members of a historic AME church in Charleston, South Carolina, were murdered by a White supremacist youth wielding a Confederate flag in June of 2015, NASCAR removed Confederate flags from official organizational spaces and asked fans to refrain from bringing the Confederate flag to NASCAR events. These timely happenings show how the historical moment is deeply entwined with cultural and structural components of our everyday social worlds and how sport and exercise become both reflective of and responsive to the major events of the current historical moment.

Appendix A

Learn More About Sociology of Sport and Physical Activity

Journals

The number of journals continues to grow in this area. The following journals are either devoted to sociology of sport or contain a high proportion of papers written from a sociological perspective.

➤ *International Review for the Sociology of Sport* (IRSS), quarterly

➤ *Sociology of Sport Journal* (SSJ), quarterly

➤ *Journal of Sport and Social Issues* (JSSI), quarterly

➤ *Culture, Sport, Society*

➤ *Leisure Studies*

➤ *Japanese Journal of Sport Sociology*

➤ *European Journal for Sport and Society*

Major Research Centers

The University of Waterloo in Canada was the first prominent center to be associated with the sociology of sport. There are now some long established research centers in North America (e.g., Universities of Alberta, Toronto, and Queens in Canada; University of Illinois and University of Iowa in the United States); Europe (e.g., University of Cologne, Germany; Loughborough University, UK); Asia (e.g., Tsukuba University, Japan; Seoul National University, South Korea); and Australasia (University of Otago, New Zealand; University of Queensland, Australia).

➤ Laboratoire APSet Sciences Sociales / Université Marc Bloch de Strasbourg (France)

➤ Sport in Society, a Northwestern University Center (www.northeastern.edu/sportinsociety)

▶ Institute for Diversity and Ethics in Sport at University of Central Florida (www.tide sport.org)

▶ Josephson Institute, Center for Sport Ethics (http://sports.josephsoninstitute.org)

▶ Tucker Center for Research on Girls and Women in Sport (www.cehd.umn.edu/tucker center)

Organizations

▶ Society of Health and Physical Educators (SHAPE America; www.shapeamerica.org)

▶ Société de Sociologie du Sport de Langue Française/French Language Society for Sport Sociology (http://3slf.fr)

▶ European Association for the Sociology of Sport (www.eass-sportsociology.eu)

▶ Japan Society of Sport Sociology (http://jsss.jp/english)

▶ North American Society for the Sociology of Sport (www.nasss.org)

▶ Nordic Sport Science Forum (http://idrottsforum.org)

▶ Program for the Advancement of Girls and Women in Sport and Physical Activity (http:// hhs.uncg.edu/wordpress/pagwspa)

Web Resources in the Sociology of Sport and Physical Activity

▶ NASSS blog (http://nasssblog.blogspot.com)

▶ One Sport Voice (www.nicolemlavoi.com)

▶ The Tennis Prof Chronicles (http://tennisprofchronicles.blogspot.com)

▶ Edge of Sports (www.edgeofsports.com)

U.S. Departments of Kinesiology Granting Doctoral Degrees in Sociology of Sport

University of Connecticut (www.uconn.edu)

▪ Program title: PhD in kinesiology
▪ Options: exercise science, sport management, and sociology of sport
▪ Department of kinesiology (http://kins.uconn.edu)

University of Georgia (www.uga.edu)

- Program title: PhD, EdD in physical education and sport studies; EdD, PhD in curriculum and instruction (pedagogy)
- Options: sport studies, motor behavior, physical education pedagogy
- Department of kinesiology (http://coe.uga.edu/directory/departments/kinesiology)

University of Houston (www.uh.edu)

- Program title: PhD in kinesiology (sociocultural influence on physical activity and obesity)
- Options: motor behavior, exercise physiology, obesity studies, sport and fitness administration
- Department of health and human performance (www.uh.edu/class/hhp)

University of Illinois at Urbana-Champaign (http://illinois.edu)

- Program title: PhD in kinesiology, PhD in community health and cultural, pedagogical and interpretive studies
- Options: health policy, epidemiology, health education, health behavior, rehabilitation, disability studies
- Department of kinesiology and community health (www.kch.uiuc.edu)

University of Kansas (www.ku.edu)

- Program title: PhD in education
- Options: health education, sports studies, biomechanics, exercise physiology
- Department of health, sport and exercise sciences (www.soe.ku.edu/depts/hses)

University of Maryland (www.umd.edu)

- Program title: PhD in kinesiology (sport commerce and culture)
- Options: cognitive motor neuroscience, exercise physiology, physical cultural studies, physical activity
- Department of kinesiology (http://sph.umd.edu/department/knes)

Springfield College (http://springfield.edu)

- Program title: PhD in movement and sport studies
- Options: physical education
- Department of exercise science and sport studies (http://springfield.edu/academic-programs/exercise-science-and-sport-studies-department)

University of Minnesota (www.umn.edu)

- Program title: PhD in kinesiology
- Options: biomechanics and neuromotor control, exercise physiology, perceptual motor control and learning, physical activity and sport science, sport management
- School of kinesiology (http://education.umn.edu/kin)

University of North Carolina at Greensboro (www.uncg.edu)

- Program titles: EdD, PhD in kinesiology (sociohistorical studies of physical activity)
- Options: applied neuromechanics, exercise physiology, motor behavior, pedagogical kinesiology, sociohistorical studies, sport and exercise psychology
- Department of kinesiology (www.uncg.edu/kin)

University of Tennessee at Knoxville (www.utk.edu)

- Program title: PhD in kinesiology and sport studies
- Options: biomechanics, exercise physiology, physical activity epidemiology, and sport psychology and motor behavior.
- Department of kinesiology and sport studies (http://krss.utk.edu)

University of Texas (www.utexas.edu)

- Program title: PhD in kinesiology
- Options: exercise science, health behavior and health education, physical culture and sport studies, sport management
- Department of kinesiology and health education (www.edb.utexas.edu/education/departments/khe/graduate/exsci)

Appendix B

Implementing Sociology of Sport and Physical Activity in Our Communities

Advocates for Ethical and Humane Sport and Physical Activity

Athletes

☐ Have you ever been on a team that came together to add their voices and actions to a local, national, or global social movement?

☐ At times, athletes can help to create the kind of fair and productive team environment that benefits all members equally. This requires thinking about the way a team is organized and resources are shared as well as how coaches, athletes, parents, sponsors, and fans interact.

☐ Star athletes are often in a position to use their elevated social status to draw attention to social issues. This requires athletes to understand their social status and be willing to use their fame to promote recognition of issues that may or may not directly affect their athletic status.

Parents

☐ In youth sport settings, parents often volunteer on league governing boards and as coaches and referees. In each of these roles, parents can be careful to address issues of access, inequalities, and community resource engagement.

☐ Parents are increasingly invited by youth sport leagues to complete a training session or sign an agreement to abide by an ethic of healthy youth sport parenting.

This typically means being supportive, refraining from yelling at youth or other fans, and contributing to an overall safe space for youth sport involvement.

☐ Elite sport programs often have a parent observation room that allows parents a space from which to view practice and training sessions but keeps them out of visual and auditory reach of the participants—the kids can neither see nor hear their parents. Use your sociological imagination to consider the benefits and pitfalls of a setting like this.

Fans

☐ Fan behavior at sporting events (youth, college, and professional) tells us how important spectatorship is for many people's identities. How can you act as a responsible fan at sporting events?

☐ Do the events you attend have codes of behavior for fans? What standards are fans held to? Do you yell negative comments and boo athletes performing on the field?

☐ Alcohol plays a factor in fan conduct, often contributing to violent and aggressive behavior. Many college and professional sporting events stop selling alcohol after a certain time to help control fan behavior.

Allied Professionals in Sport and Physical Activity

Shop Owners

☐ What sort of goods and services do you offer? How are they connected to sport and exercise?

☐ Advertising your store and its products is important for your success. Do you use certain athletes to promote the values of your store and products?

☐ Do you sell sizes that represent the spectrum of movers, or are you focused on a certain body type?

☐ Do you sponsor youth teams? In what sports? For boys and girls? In what neighborhoods?

Journalists

☐ What sports and teams do you cover?

☐ How do you advocate for athletes who are marginalized? Or sports that traditionally receive less media coverage?

☐ Think about the adjectives you use to describe athletes. Work to avoid words that highlight an athlete in stereotypical gendered or racialized phrases.

☐ Do your homework on the history of the sport, athletes, and communities you are writing about.

☐ Think about reader comments. Do you allow a space for anonymous readers to leave comments about athletes that are personal attacks? Make your column or articles a space where identified readers can engage with each other about ideas.

Worksite Wellness Coordinators

☐ How can you promote wellness for people who have traditionally been underserved in exercise and sport settings?

☐ Use posters and images in your work space to represent a diversity of movers—both sexes and all shapes, ages, and races.

☐ Contribute to the development of a healthy workspace by promoting physical activity as a means to relax, grow in confidence, and achieve outcomes based on each individual's needs rather than achievement-oriented competition.

Coach

☐ Write your coaching philosophy and share it with your athletes and their parents.

☐ If you work with youth athletes, develop a communication plan with their parents.

☐ Work to ensure that the safety of your athletes is primary, even if the outcome of the game is affected.

☐ Work to ensure that you do not engage in name calling as a form of motivation.

☐ Attend coaching clinics and workshops to develop your philosophy, style, and strategies.

☐ Set a good example for athletes during the game by respecting game officials and the rules of the sport.

Physical Educator

☐ Establish a space where all students are safe and feel valued as participants. Physical education is a space that is often rife with bullying. Develop strategies to eliminate bullying from your classes.

☐ Attend to the needs of all your students, from the low-skilled and unmotivated to the low-skilled but highly motivated to the more elite movers, who will also vary in their motivation.

☐ Promote gender equity in your classroom by offering a range of sport and physical activities that every student participates in.

☐ Celebrate the sporting cultures of the students in your class by incorporating games and activities from other countries and cultures.

☐ Come up with a variety of ways of picking teams that do not emphasize skill or sex.

☐ Be sure to use vocabulary that avoids demeaning your students and their bodies and performances.

☐ Find ways to engage your students that do not focus on social comparison and competition.

Fitness Leader

☐ Think about ways to motivate movers that does not rely on negative or degrading language.

☐ Use music that represents the participants in your classes.

☐ Be open to finding modifications for movers who may be restricted by their body size or abilities.

Physical Therapist

☐ Ask your clients questions about their interests in sport and exercise to help develop a program suitable for their motivations.

☐ Remind yourself that your clients have feelings. Part of your work with them will be helping them to feel more comfortable and confident in a body that has undergone an injury or accident.

Athletic Trainer

☐ The safety of your athletes is paramount. Develop a protocol for communicating with coaches and athletes that puts the safety of the athlete above all other factors.

☐ Create a support group for injured athletes to help them cope with the change in their athletic identity and perhaps their changing role on their team.

League Directors

☐ Develop a transparent communication plan for coaches and parents as well as athletes.

☐ Schedule games that do not privilege one level or sex over another.

☐ Require coaches to attend training programs and certifications.

☐ Require parents to attend orientations.

☐ Provide life skills for your athletes to help prepare them for their postplaying career.

Academic Professionals

Professors and Faculty

☐ Be a good colleague by talking with faculty members in a variety of departments about the ways you can support one another and what you all do.

☐ Provide readings for your students that reflect diversity (e.g., diversity of authors but also the populations studied).

☐ Address topics in your classes that challenge students to think about the ways the subdisciplines can work together and how students in different fields can learn from each other.

Directors of Research Centers

☐ Include a variety of scholars on your advisory board that reflect diverse ideas and backgrounds.

☐ Do a needs assessment in your community to see how your center might engage with the local population.

Directors of Coaching Education

☐ Develop policies and practices for communicating with athletes and parents.

☐ Train coaches in developing their own coaching philosophy that helps them think about the role of winning, skill development, character development, and player safety.

Directors of Sport Policy Institutes

☐ Develop critical partnerships with major sport governing organizations. Be willing to work in collaboration to continually enhance the positive outcomes of sport in communities and for individuals.

☐ Create and disseminate reports on the social, economic, political, and environmental influence of sport and physical activity programs and spaces.

☐ Host public conversations about best practices and community concerns regarding sport and physical activity programs, venues, and events.

Directors of Campus Recreation

- ☐ Offer a range of sports that meet the needs of your student population.
- ☐ Offer a schedule that does not privilege one sport or sex.
- ☐ If you offer coed teams, consider how you will ensure the full participation of both sexes.
- ☐ Hire and train referees who reflect the diversity of your student population.
- ☐ Develop recruitment strategies to reach underserved populations on your campus.

References

Adams, M.L. (2011). *Artistic impressions: Figure skating, masculinity, and the limits of sport.* Toronto, Ontario, Canada: University of Toronto Press.

Anderson, B. (1983). *Imagined communities. Reflections on the origin and spread of nationalism.* London, England: Verso.

Andrews, D.L. (2008). Kinesiology's inconvenient truth and the physical cultural studies imperative. *Quest, 60,* 46-63.

Annan, K. (2004, November 5). Declaration of the UN Secretary-General at the launch of the International Year of Sport and Physical Education, 2005. United Nations headquarters, New York, NY.

Appadurai, A. (1990). Disjuncture and difference in the global cultural economy. *Theory, Culture & Society, 7,* 295-310.

Babiash, P., Porcari, J.P., Steffen, J., Doberstein, S., & Foster, C. (2013, November). Crossfit: New research puts popular workout to the test. American Council on Exercise. Retrieved from www.acefitness.org/prosourcearticle/3542/crossfit-sup-tm-sup-new-research-puts-popular

Baca Zinn, M., Hondagneu-Sotelo, P., & Messner, M. (2010). *Gender through the prism of difference* (4th ed.). New York, NY: Oxford University Press.

Bairner, A. (2001). *Sport, nationalism and globalization: European and North American perspectives.* Albany, NY: SUNY Press.

Birrell, S., & Cole, C.L. (1994). *Women, sport, and culture.* Champaign, IL: Human Kinetics.

Bissinger, H.G. (1990). *Friday night lights: A town, a team, and a dream.* Boston, MA: De Capo Press.

Bourdieu, P. (1986) The forms of capital. In J. Richardson (Ed.), *Handbook of theory and research for the sociology of education* (pp. 241-258). New York: Greenwood.

Boyle, R.H. (1963). *Sport: Mirror of American life.* Boston, MA: Little & Brown.

Brooks, D.D. (1984). The current status of sport sociology within American and Canadian colleges and universities. Paper presented at the Olympic Scientific Congress Meeting (Eugene, OR).

Brownell, K., & Horgen, K.B. (2004). *Food fight: The inside story of the food industry, America's obesity crisis, and what we can do about it.* New York, NY: McGraw-Hill.

Bruce, T. (2014). Us and them: The influence of discourses of nationalism on media coverage of the Paralympics. *Disability & Society, 29*(9), 1443-1459.

Burrows, L., & Wright, J. (2004). The discursive production of childhood, identity and health. In J. Evans, B. Davies, & J. Wright (Eds.), *Body knowledge and control: Studies in the sociology of education and physical culture* (pp. 83-95). London, England: Routledge.

Buysse, J.M., & Embser-Herbert, M.S. (2004). Constructions of gender in sport: An analysis of intercollegiate media guide cover photographs. *Gender & Society, 18*(1), 166-181.

Casper, M.J., & Currah, P. (2011). *Corpus: An interdisciplinary reader on bodies and knowledge.* New York, NY: Palgrave Macmillan.

Chen, T. (2012). From the 'Taiwan Yankees' to the New York Yankees. *Sociology of Sport Journal, 29,* 546-558.

Coakley, J.J. (2009). *Sports in society: Issues and controversies* (10th ed.). Boston, MA: McGraw Hill.

Coakley, J.J. (2011). Youth sports: What counts as "positive development"? *Journal of Sport and Social Issues, 35*(3), 306-324.

Collier, J., Rosaldo, M.Z., & Yanagisako, S. (1992). Is there a family? New anthropological views. In B. Thorne & M. Yalom (Eds.), *Rethinking the family: Some feminist questions* (pp. 31-48). Boston, MA: Northeastern University Press.

Connell, R.W. (1990). An iron man: The body and some contradictions of hegemonic masculinity. In M.A. Messner & D.E. Sabo (Eds.), *Sport, men and the gender order: Critical feminist perspectives* (pp. 83-96). Champaign, IL: Human Kinetics.

Cunningham, G.B., & Regan, M.R., Jr. (2011). Political activism, racial identity and the commercial endorsement of athletes. *International Review for the Sociology of Sport, 47*(6), 657-669.

Darnell, S. (2010). Power, politics and "sport for development and peace": Investigating the utility of sport for international development. *Sociology of Sport Journal, 27*(1), 54-75.

De la Porta, D., & Diani, M. (2006). *Social movements: An introduction* (2nd ed.). Malden, MA: Blackwell.

DeLuca, J.R. (2013). Submersed in social segregation: The (re)production of social capital through swim club membership. *Journal of Sport and Social Issues, 37*(4), 340-363.

DePauw, K., & Gavron, S. (2005). *Disability sport* (2nd ed.). Champaign, IL: Human Kinetics.

Douglas, D.D. (2002). Venus, Serena, and the Women's Tennis Association (WTA): When and where "race" enters. *Sociology of Sport Journal, 22*(3), 256-282.

Duncan, M.C. (1994). The politics of women's body images and practices: Foucault, the panopticon, and *Shape* magazine. *Journal of Sport and Social Issues, 18*(1), 48-65.

Duncan, M.C., & Jamieson, K.M. (2012). Sociology of physical activity. In S.J. Hoffman (Ed.), *Introduction to kinesiology* (pp. 183-208). Champaign, IL: Human Kinetics.

Duquin, M. (1994). The body snatchers and Dr. Frankenstein revisited: Social construction and deconstruction of bodies and sport. *Journal of Sport and Social Issues, 18*(3), 268-281.

Dworkin, S.L., & Wachs, F.L. (2000). Disciplining the body. HIV-positive male athletes, media surveillance, and the policing of sexuality. In S. Birrell & M.G. McDonald (Eds.), *Reading sport: Critical essay in power and representation* (pp. 251-278). Boston, MA: Northeastern University Press.

Eitzen, D.S. (2002). *Fair and foul: Beyond the myths and paradoxes of sport* (2nd ed.). Lanham, MD: Rowman & Littlefield.

Eitzen, D.S. (2012). *Fair and foul: Beyond the myths and paradoxes of sport* (5th ed.). Lanham, MD: Rowman & Littlefield.

Eitzen, D.S., & Baca Zinn, M. (1989). The de-athleticization of women: The naming and gender marking of collegiate sport teams. *Sociology of Sport Journal, 6*, 362-370.

Eitzen, D.S., & Furst, D. (1989). Racial bias in women's collegiate volleyball. *Journal of Sport and Social Issues, 13*, 46-51.

Eitzen, D.S., & Sage, G.H. (2008). *Sociology of North American sport* (8th ed.). Boulder, CO: Paradigm.

Elliott, R., & Weedon, G. (2011). Foreign players in the English Premier Academy League: 'Feet drain' or 'feet exchange'? *International Review for the Sociology of Sport, 46*(1), 61-75.

Enloe, C. (2004). *The curious feminist: Searching for women in a new age of empire*. Berkeley, CA: University of California Press.

Evans, J., Davies, B., & Wright, J. (2004). *Body knowledge and control: Studies in the sociology of physical education and health*. London, England: Routledge.

Fisher, M. (2015). Women of color and the gender wage gap. Center for American Progress. Retrieved from www.americanprogress.org/issues/women/report/2015/04/14/110962/women-of-color-and-the-gender-wage-gap

Foley, D.E. (1999). High school football: Deep in the heart of South Tejas. In J. Coakley & P. Donnelly (Eds.), *Inside sports* (pp. 133-138). New York, NY: Routledge.

Freund, P. (2001). Bodies, disability and spaces: The social model and disabling spatial organizations. *Disability and Society, 16*(5), 689-706.

Gard, M., & Wright, J. (2006). *The obesity epidemic: Science, morality and ideology*. London, England: Routledge.

Gardiner, G. (2003). Running for country: Australian Print Media Representation of Indigenous Athletes in the 27th Olympiad. *Journal of Sport and Social Issues, 27*(3), 233-260.

Geertz, C. (1973). *The interpretation of cultures*. New York, NY: Basic Books.

Giardina, M. (2005). *Sporting pedagogies: Performing culture and identity in the global arena*. New York, NY: Peter Lang.

Glauber, B. (2013, November 29). Richie Incognito-Jonathan Martin hazing story puts NFL locker room behavior in spotlight. *Newsday*. Retrieved from www.newsday.com/sports/football/richie-incognito-jonathan-martin-hazing-story-puts-nfl-locker-room-behavior-in-spotlight-1.6411732

González, G.L. (1996). The stacking of Latinos in Major League Baseball: A forgotten minority? *Journal of Sport and Social Issues, 20*(2), 134-160.

González, G.L. (2002). The stacking of Latinos in Major League Baseball: Does it matter if a player is drafted? *Journal of Hispanic Higher Education, 1*(4), 320-328.

Greendorfer, S.L. (1977). Sociology of sport: Knowledge of what. *Quest, 28*(1), 58-65. DOI: 10.1080/00336297.1977.10519900

Greendorfer, S. (1983). Shaping the female athlete: The impact of the family. In M.A. Boutilier & L. San Giovanni (Eds.), *The sporting woman* (pp. 135-146). Champaign, IL: Human Kinetics.

Gremillion, H. (2005). The cultural politics of body size. *Annual Review of Anthropology, 34*, 13-32.

Hargreaves, J.A., & Vertinsky, P. (2007). *Physical culture, power, and the body*. London, England: Routledge.

Hegewisch, A., Williams, C., Hartmann, H., & Hudiberg, S.K. (2014). Fact sheet: The gender wage gap: 2013. Differences by race and ethnicity. Retrieved from www.iwpr.org/publications/pubs/the-gender-wage-gap-2013-differences-by-race-and-ethnicity-no-growth-in-real-wages-for-women

Herndon, A. (2002). Disparate but disabled: Fat embodiment and disability studies. *NWSA Journal, 14*(3), 120-137.

Howson, A., & Inglis, D. (2001). The body in sociology: Tensions inside and outside sociological thought. *The Sociological Review, 49*(3), 297-317.

Husted Harper, I. (1898). *The life and work of Susan B. Anthony: Including public addresses, her own letters and many from her contemporaries during 50 years*. Indianapolis, IN: Brown-Merrill.

Huizinga, J. (1949). *Homo ludens: A study of the play-element in culture*. London, England: Routledge & Kegan Paul. (Original work published in Dutch in 1938.)

Jackson, S.J., Batty, R., & Scherer, J. (2001). Transnational sport marketing at the global/local nexus: The Adidasification of the New Zealand All Blacks. *International Journal of Sports Marketing & Sponsorship, 3*(2), 185.

Jackson, S., & Hokowhitu, B. (2005). Sport, tribes, and technology: The New Zealand All Blacks *Haka* and the politics of identity. In M. Silk, D.L. Andrews, & C.L. Cole (Eds.), *Sport and corporate nationalisms* (pp. 66-82). London, England: Bloomsbury Academic Press.

Jamieson, K.M., Stringer, A.J., & Andrews, M.B. (2008). Athletic fatness: Forgiving corpulence in elite bodies. *Sociology of Sport Journal, 25*(1), 148-163.

Johnson, B.D., & Johnson, N.R. (1995). Stacking and "stoppers": A test of the outcome control hypothesis. *Sociology of Sport Journal, 12*, 105-112.

Kane, M.J., & Greendorfer, S.L. (1994). The media's role in accommodating and resisting stereotyped images of women in sport. In P.J. Creedon (Ed.), *Women, media and sport: Challenging gender values* (pp. 28-44). Thousand Oaks, CA: Sage.

Kenyon, G.S., & Loy, J.W. (1965). Toward a sociology of sport. *JOPERD, 36*(5), 24-25; 68-69.

Kidd, B. (2010). Epilogue: The struggle must continue. *Sport in Society, 13*(1), 157-165.

King, S. (2005). Marketing generosity: The Avon Worldwide Fund for Women's Health and the reinvention of global corporate citizenship. In M. Silk, D.L. Andrews, & C.L. Cole (Eds.), *Sport and corporate nationalisms* (pp. 83-108). London, England: Bloomsbury Academic Press.

King, S. (2009). Virtually normal: Mark Bingham, the war on terror, and the sexual politics of sport. *Journal of Sport and Social Issues, 33*(1), 5-24.

Klein, A. (2006). *Growing the game: The globalization of Major League Baseball*. New Haven, CT: Yale University Press.

Klein, C. (2012). Nine things you may not know about Wimbledon. Retrieved from www.history.com/news/9-things-you-may-not-know-about-wimbledon

Kurtzleben, D. (2013, June 20). Up and running: The rise of the themed road race. *US News and World Report*. Retrieved from www.usnews.com/news/articles/2013/06/20/how-tough-mudder-the-color-run-and-the-rock-n-roll-marathon-are-leading-a-new-pack-of-themed-races

Kusz, K.W. (2007). From NASCAR nation to Pat Tillman: Notes on sport and politics of White cultural nationalism in post-9/11 America. *Journal of Sport and Social Issues, 31*(1), 77-88.

Lauff, J. (2011). Participation rates of developing countries in international disability sport: A summary and the importance of statistics for understanding and planning. *Sport in Society: Cultures, Commerce, Media, Politics, 14*(9), 1280-1284.

Lim, S-Y. (2009). Racial and sexual discrimination occurring to Korean players on the USLPGA tour. (Unpublished doctoral dissertation). University of Tennessee, Knoxville.

Longest, K.C. (2008). Teaching the sociology of sport: A collection of syllabi, assignments, and other resources (5th ed.). Washington, DC: ASA.

Longhurst, R. (2005). Fat bodies: Developing geographical research agendas. *Progress Human Geography, 29*(3), 247-259.

Loy, J.W., & Kenyon, G.S. (1969). *Sport, culture, and society: A reader on the sociology of sport*. Toronto, Ontario, Canada: Macmillan.

Luschen, R.F.G., & Sage, G.H. (1981). *Handbook of social science of sport*. Champaign, IL: Stipes.

Macionis, J.J. (2001). *Society: The basics* (6th ed.). Upper Saddle River, NJ: Pearson Prentice Hall.

Maguire, J. (2005). *Power and global sport: Zones of prestige, emulation and resistance*. London, England: Routledge.

MARGARET Fund of National Women's Law Center. (n.d.). Title IX info. Retrieved from www.titleix.info

Markula, P. (1995). Firm but shapely, fit but sexy, strong but thin: The postmodern aerobicizing female bodies. *Sociology of Sport Journal, 12*, 424-453.

McAlaster, T. (2013, October 11). How much does it cost to race an Ironman? *The Globe and Mail.* Retrieved from www.theglobeandmail.com/sports/more-sports/i-am-ironman/article14815416

McDonald, M.G., & Birrell, S. (1999). Reading sport critically: A methodology for interrogating power. *Sociology of Sport Journal, 16*(4), 283-300.

Messner, M. (2000). Becoming 100% straight. In M. Baca-Zinn, P. Hondagneu-Sotelo, & M.A. Messner (Eds.), *Gender through the prism of difference* (pp. 205-210). Boston, MA: Allyn & Bacon.

Miller, F.D. (1999). The end of SDS and the emergence of weatherman: Demise through success. In J. Freeman & V. Johnson (Eds.), *Waves of protest: Social movements since the sixties* (pp. 303-324). Lanham, MD: Rowman & Littlefield.

Mills, C.W. (2004). The sociological imagination. (Originally published in 1959). In Howard, E.L. (Ed.), *Classic readings in sociology,* 3rd ed. (pp. 1-6). Belmont, CA: Wadsworth.

Moore, L.J., & Kosut, M. (2010). *The body reader: Essential cultural and social readings.* New York, NY: New York University Press.

Nixon, H.L. (2010). Sport sociology, NASSS, and undergraduate education in the United States: A social network perspective for developing the field. *Sociology of Sport Journal, 27*, 76-88.

Noll, R.G., & Zimbalist, A.S. (1997). *Sports, jobs, and taxes: The economic impact of sports teams and stadiums.* Washington, DC: The Brookings Institute.

O'Connor, A. (2011). A marathon runner delivers a baby. The New York Times. Retrieved from http://well.blogs.nytimes.com/2011/10/11/a-marathon-runner-delivers-a-baby/?_r=0

Omi, M., & Winant, H. (1994). *Racial formation in the United States: From the 1960s to the 1990s* (2nd ed.). New York, NY: Routledge.

Organisation for Economic Co-operation and Development. (2016). Hours worked: Average annual hours actually worked. *OECD Employment and Labour Market Statistics* [database]. DOI: http://dx.doi.org/10.1787/data-00303-en

Palmer, C. (2001). Outside the imagined community: Basque terrorism, political activism, and the Tour de France. *Sociology of Sport Journal, 18*(2), 143-161.

Pescador, J.J. (2004). ¡Vamos taximora! Mexican/Chicano soccer associations and transnational/translocal communities, 1967–2002. *Latino Studies, 2,* 352–376.

Promis, D., Erevelles, N., & Matthews, J. (2001). Reconceptualizing inclusion: The politics of university sports and recreation programs for students with mobility impairments. *Sociology of Sport Journal, 18,* 37-50.

Purdue, D.E.J., & Howe, P.D. (2013). Who's in and who is out? Legitimate bodies within the Paralympic Games. *Sociology of Sport Journal, 30,* 24-40.

Regalado, S. (1998). *Viva baseball! Latin Major Leaguers and their special hunger* (2nd ed.). Champaign, IL: University of Illinois Press.

Rice, E. (1929). *A brief history of physical education.* New York, NY: A.S. Barnes.

Ripley, A. (2013, 18 September). The case against high-school sports. *The Atlantic.* Retrieved from www.theatlantic.com/magazine/archive/2013/10/the-case-against-high-school-sports/309447

Robertson, R. (1992). *Globalization: Social theory and global culture.* London, England: Sage.

Roderick, M.J. (2012). An unpaid labor of love: Professional footballers, family life, and the problem of job relocation. *Journal of Sport and Social Issues, 36*(3), 317-338.

Ronca, D. (2010). How the Nike+ Human Race works. Retrieved from http://adventure.howstuffworks.com/outdoor-activities/running/events/nike-human-race.htm

Ruihley, B.J., & Billings, A.C. (2012). Infiltrating the boys' club: Motivations for women's fantasy sport participation. *International Review for the Sociology of Sport, 48*(4), 435-452.

Rumford, C. (2007). More than a game: Globalization and the post-westernization of world cricket. *Global Networks, 7*(2), 202-214.

Sabo, D., & Veliz, P. (2008). *Go out and play: Youth sports in America.* East Meadow, NY: Women's Sports Foundation.

Sage, G.H. (1998). Power and ideology in North American sport: A critical perspective (2nd ed.). Champaign, IL: Human Kinetics.

Sage, G.H. (2010). *Globalizing sport: How organizations, corporations, media, and politics are changing sport.* St. Paul, MN: Paradigm.

Schimmel, K.S. (2012). Protecting the NFL/militarizing the homeland: Citizen soldiers and urban resilience in post-9/11 America. *International Review for the Sociology of Sport, 47*(3), 338-357.

Scritchfield, R. (2012, October 29). Myths and facts: Exercising while pregnant. *US News and World Report*. Retrieved from http://health.usnews.com/health-news/blogs/eat-run/2012/10/29/myths-and-facts-exercising-while-pregnant

Shilling, C. (2005). *The body in culture, technology & society*. Thousand Oaks, CA: Sage.

Shilling, C. (2008). *Changing bodies: Habit, crisis and creativity*. London, England: Sage.

Shin, E.H., & Nam, E.A. (2004). Culture, gender roles, and sport: The case of Korean players on the USLPGA tour. *Journal of Sport and Social Issues, 28*, 223-244.

Shontel, A. (2011, February 24). 15 seriously disturbing facts about your job. *Business Insider*. Retrieved from www.businessinsider.com/disturbing-facts-about-your-job-2011-2

Simons, H.D. (2003). Race and penalized sports behaviors. *International Review for the Sociology of Sport, 38*(1), 5-22.

Smith, B. (2013). Sporting spinal cord injuries, social relations, and rehabilitation narratives: An ethnographic, creative non-fiction of becoming disabled through sport. *Sociology of Sport Journal, 30*, 132-152.

Smith, M., & Wrynn, A. (2010). Women in the 2010 Olympic and Paralympic Games: An analysis of participation, leadership and media opportunities. East Meadow, NY: Women's Sports Foundation

Smith, M.M., & Wrynn, A.M. (2013). Women in the 2012 Olympic and Paralympic Games: An analysis of participation and leadership opportunities. A Women's Sports Foundation research report. East Meadow, NY: Women's Sports Foundation, and SHARP Center, University of Michigan.

Snyder, E. E., & Sprietzer, E. (1979). Sport sociology and the discipline of sociology: Present status and speculations about the future. Paper presented at Annual Meeting of the American Sociological Association (Boston, MA).

Sport England. (n.d.). Sport and disability. Retrieved from www.sportengland.org/research/encouraging-take-up/key-influences/sport-and-disability

Stone, E. (2001). Disability, sport, and the body in China. *Sociology of Sport Journal, 18*(1), 51-68.

Thomas, J. (2008). AAKPE survey of doctoral programs. *Kinesiology Today, 1*(1), 2.

Thompson, S.M. (1999). *Mother's taxi: Sport and women's labor*. Albany, NY: SUNY.

Thorne, B. (1992). Feminism and the family: Two decades of thought. In B. Thorne & M. Yalom (Eds.), *Rethinking the family: Some feminist questions* (pp. 3-30). Boston, MA: Northeastern University Press.

Thorne, B. (1993). *Gender play: Girls and boys in school*. New Brunswick, NJ: Rutgers University Press.

Title IX, Education Amendments of 1972. Retrieved from www.dol.gov/oasam/regs/statutes/titleix.htm

Travers, A., & Deri, J. (2010). Transgender inclusion and the changing face of lesbian softball leagues. *International Review for the Sociology of Sport, 46*(4), 488-507.

Trujillo, N. (1995). Machines, missiles, and men: Images of the male body on ABC's Monday Night Football. *Sociology of Sport Journal, 12*(4), 403-423.

UN creates International Day of Sport for Development and Peace. (2013). Retrieved from www.olympic.org/news/un-creates-international-day-of-sport-for-development-and-peace/207997

United Nations Enable. (n.d.). Factsheet on persons with disabilities. Retrieved from www.un.org/disabilities/default.asp?id=18#text

U.S. Department of Health and Human Services. (2010). *The Surgeon General's vision for a healthy and fit nation*. Rockville, MD: U.S. Department of Health and Human Services, Office of the Surgeon General.

U.S. Department of Labor, Bureau of Labor Statistics. (2015). Occupational outlook handbook, 2014-15. Retrieved from www.bls.gov/ooh/personal-care-and-service/fitness-trainers-and-instructors.htm

Ver Ploeg, M., Mancino, L., Todd, J.E., Clay, D.M., & Scharadin, B. (2015). Where do Americans usually shop for food and how do they travel to get there? Initial findings from the National Household Food Acquisition and Purchase Survey. Economic Information Bulletin 138. Retrieved from www.ers.usda.gov/media/1807325/eib138.pdf

Wheaton, B. (2013). *The cultural politics of lifestyle sports*. London, England: Routledge.

Whyte, W.F. (1955). *Street corner society*. Expanded edition (Originally published in 1943). Chicago, IL: University of Chicago Press.

Zirin, D. (2013). *Game over: How politics has turned the sports world upside down*. New York, NY: The New Press.

Zirin, D. (2014). *Brazil's dance with the devil: The World Cup, the Olympics, and the fight for democracy*. Chicago, IL: Haymarket Books.

Index

Note: The italicized *f* and *t* following page numbers refer to figures and tables, respectively.

About the Authors

Katherine M. Jamieson is a professor in the department of kinesiology and health science at California State University at Sacramento. Dr. Jamieson's research interests include various issues related to sport, power, and social stratification. Her most current research interests include transnational feminist and postcolonial analyses of physical culture, with specific interest in the LPGA and global and transnational conditions of elite sport settings as well as more local engagements in physical activity and social issues. Dr. Jamieson is a regular reviewer for the *Journal of Sport and Social Issues*, *Women in Sport and Physical Activity Journal*, and *Research Quarterly for Exercise and Sport*. Courses she regularly teaches are Sport in Society: Race, Class, and Gender; Sport in Society: Global and Ethnic Relations; Qualitative Inquiry in Health and Human Performance; and Sport and Feminisms. Dr. Jamieson's research has been published in *Sociology of Sport Journal*; *Journal of Sport and Social Issues*; *Avante, Women in Sport and Physical Activity Journal*; *Journal of Physical Education, Recreation and Dance*; *Reading Sport: Critical Essays on Power and Representation*; and *Contemporary Issues in Sociology of Sport*.

Photo courtesy University of North Carolina at Greensboro.

Maureen M. Smith is a professor in the department of kinesiology and health science at California State University at Sacramento. Dr. Smith's research interests include examining racial issues in sport and material culture related to sport, specifically sport statues and monuments. She is the coauthor (with Rita Liberti) of the book *(Re)Presenting Wilma Rudolph*. Dr. Smith is a regular reviewer for *International Journal of the History of Sport*. Courses she regularly teaches are Sociology of Sport, History and Philosophy of Sport and Physical Education, and Sport in Society. Her research has been published in the *Journal of Sport and Social Issues*, *Journal of Sport History*, *Sport and Society*, and *International Journal of the History of Sport*. Dr. Smith is a past president of the North American Society for Sport History.

© Maureen M. Smith.

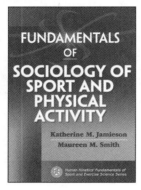
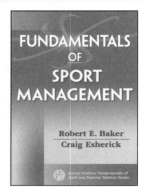